MULTAS PER G

A COLLECTION OF LATIN PASSAGES SELECTED FROM HISTORY, PROSE, AND POETRY

COMPILED AND EDITED BY PAUL WHALEN

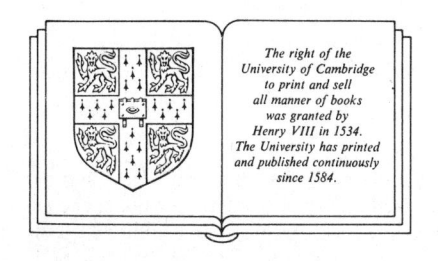

CAMBRIDGE UNIVERSITY PRESS
Cambridge
New York   Port Chester   Melbourne   Sydney

THEMES IN LATIN LITERATURE

amor et amicitia
imperium et civitas
multas per gentes
urbs antiqua

Published by the Press Syndicate of the University of Cambridge
The Pitt Building, Trumpington Street, Cambridge CB2 1RP
40 West 20th Street, New York, NY 10011, USA
10 Stamford Road, Oakleigh, Melbourne 3166, Australia

© Irwin Publishing Inc., Canada, 1989

First published 1989 by Irwin Publishing Inc., Canada

This edition first published 1989

Printed in Great Britain at the University Press, Cambridge

British Library Cataloguing in Publication Data

Multas per gentes: a collection of Latin
   passages selected from history, poetry,
   speeches, inscriptions and letters with
   vocabulary, notes and questions
   1. Latin language – Readers
   I. Whalen, Paul
   478.6'421

Library of Congress Cataloging-in-Publication Data

Multas per gentes: a collection of Latin passages selected from
   history, poetry, speeches, inscriptions, and letters, with
   vocabulary, notes, and questions/compiled and edited by Paul
   Whalen.
First published in 1989 by Irwin Publishing Inc., Canada – T.p.
   verso.
   English and Latin.
   Includes bibliographies.
   1. Latin language – Readers – Geography.   2. Geography,
   Ancient – Sources.   3. Travel, Ancient – Sources.   4. Voyages
   to the otherworld.   5. Latin literature.
   I. Whalen, Paul.
   PA2095.M85   1989
   478.6'421 – dc19

ISBN 0 521 37738 2

Cover Photograph: The cover shows a detail of Alexander the Great and his horse, Bucephalas, from a mosaic in the National Museum, Naples. Alexander the Great not only represents the common traveller in Classical times – the soldier who overcame fears and obstacles on land and water in his quest to conquer, explore, and civilize. He also symbolizes the romantic adventurer who looks for more worlds to see and conquer. Courtesy The Bettmann Archive, Inc.

Maps and illustrations by Tibor Kovalik

Text and cover design by Brant Cowie/Artplus Ltd.
Typeset by Jay Tee Graphics Ltd.

Table of Contents

Note to the Teacher VIII
To the Student IX
Glossary of Some Literary Terms Used in *Themes in Latin Literature* X
Short Biographies of Latin Authors Quoted in *multas per gentes* XII
Introduction XVI

	No. of Lines	Page
PART I: GEOGRAPHY, CUSTOMS, AND PEOPLE		1
The Geography of India	21	2
Curtius, *Historiae Alexandri* VIII.ix.13-19; IX.i.9-12		
The Hercynian Forest of Germany	13	2
Caesar, *De Bello Gallico* VI.25-28		
The People of India	16	4
Curtius, *Historiae Alexandri* VIII.ix.20-35		
The People of Germany	21	4
Caesar, *De Bello Gallico* VI.21-22		
The Druids	20	6
Caesar, *De Bello Gallico* VI.14		
Human Sacrifices	16	6
Caesar, *De Bello Gallico* VI.16		
The Druid Stronghold of Anglesey	17	8
Tacitus, *Annals* XIV.29-30		
Achaemenides and Polyphemus		
I Achaemenides Tells His Story	37	10
Vergil, *Aeneid* III.616-654		
II The Trojans Escape from the Cyclopes	30	12
Vergil, *Aeneid* III.655-683		
Initial Questions		14
Discussion Questions		15
Further Readings		15

	No. of Lines	Page

PART II: ANCIENT SITES 17

The Hanging Gardens of Babylon	30	18
Curtius, *Historiae Alexandri* V.i.24-36		
A Roman General Visits the Sites of Greece	41	20
Livy, *Ab Urbe Condita* XLV.27-28		
Initial Questions		22
Discussion Questions		22
Further Readings		22

PART III: TRAVEL BY LAND, WATER, AND AIR 23

A Roman Governor Tours His Province	22	24
Cicero, In *Verrem* II.v.26-27		
Hannibal Crosses the Alps	37	26
Livy, *Ab Urbe Condita* XXI.35-37		
Oceanus		
I The Tide Scatters the Fleet	37	28
Curtius, *Historiae Alexandri* IX.ix.3-17		
II Recovery and Reaching the Goal	39	30
Curtius, *Historiae Alexandri* IX.ix.18-27		
Alexander's Journey in the Desert	34	32
Curtius, *Historiae Alexandri* IX.x.8-18		
Horace's Journey to Brundisium	24	34
Horace, *Satires* I.v.1-26		
Julius Caesar's First Invasion of Britain		
I Invasion Preparations and the Channel Crossing	18	36
Caesar, *De Bello Gallico* IV.23		
II Difficulties in Landing	14	36
Caesar, *De Bello Gallico* IV.24		
III The Landing	18	38
Caesar, *De Bello Gallico* IV.25		
IV Caesar Wins Control	15	38
Caesar, *De Bello Gallico* IV.26		
Daedalus and Icarus		
I Preparations for the Flight	26	40
Ovid, *Metamorphoses* VIII.183-209		
II The Flight	26	42
Ovid, *Metamorphoses* VIII.210-235		

	No. of Lines	Page
Initial Questions		44
Discussion Questions		46
Further Readings		47

PART IV: A JOURNEY THROUGH THE UNDERWORLD
(Selections from Vergil's *Aeneid*, Book Six)

49

	No. of Lines	Page
The Descent to the Underworld	32	50
Lines 124-155		
The Portals of Hades	27	52
Lines 268-294		
Charon, Ferryman of the Dead	19	54
Lines 298-316		
Cerberus	9	54
Lines 417-425		
Tartarus	35	56
Lines 548-562; 608-627		
Elysium	29	58
Lines 637-665		
The Pageant of Heroes	17	60
Lines 788-797; 847-853		
The Gates of Sleep	7	60
Lines 893-899		
Initial Questions		62
Discussion Questions		63
Further Readings		64

DEDICATION

For the Latin teachers of Ontario, as many as there have been, are and will be

ACKNOWLEDGEMENT

The author would like to thank

Professor Alexander Dalzell
Trinity College
University of Toronto
Toronto, Ontario

whose advice and comments were particularly helpful in preparing *multas per gentes*.

NOTE TO THE TEACHER

It is intended that this text will provide you with suitable readings for an examination of the theme of *multas per gentes*.

Over 400 lines are offered here. Additional passages are listed for further exploration of the theme since space limitations have prevented the inclusion of further suitable passages.

Since each selection is a self-contained unit with its own vocabulary and notes, there is no need to read every selection, nor to read each in the order given here. I have attempted to include a variety of genres and authors and of passages known and not so well known, long and short, serious and humorous, easy and difficult.

The questions at the end of each subtopic are intended to be directional, not comprehensive, and can readily be adjusted to suit your prose and poetry readings. The questions are designed to explore the surface meaning of passages, to compare the effectiveness of one literary piece with another in a subtopic, to develop a deeper understanding of the subtopic and its relationship to the general theme of travel and adventure.

The metre used by all the poets in this book is dactylic hexameter.

The Latin readings are either unadapted or very mildly adapted; adaptation usually consists of deletion rather than alteration.

To the Student

The notes and vocabulary should assist you in translating each passage. To appreciate the relationship of sound to sense, an oral reading, in both prose and poetry, is essential not only at the initial exploration but also at the end with your discussion and analysis.

The metre used by all the poets—Vergil, Horace, and Ovid—in *multas per gentes* is dactylic hexameter.

The initial questions at the end of each subtopic are intended to help consolidate comprehension after you have worked through the passage beforehand. An analysis of the writer's treatment of the theme is expected in your class discussion. Many questions require you to quote from the Latin text words and phrases that support your viewpoint.

The discussion questions are designed to compare and contrast the different writers' concepts of the theme and their effectiveness and distinctiveness as writers; to help you understand the subtopic and its relationship to the theme; and, finally, to form analogies between the ancient Roman and today's traveller.

Many questions do not have clear-cut "correct" answers, and are intended to provoke discussion. In this way, you will learn more about the didactic and aesthetic aspects of the theme.

Glossary of Some Literary Terms Used in *Themes in Latin Literature*

In writing a literary appreciation for a piece of literature, it is not enough simply to list literary devices and examples. Always examine critically each device to see *how* the writer uses it and *what* effect is achieved by its use in that context.

anaphora: the repetition of an important word at the beginning of several successive clauses

alliteration: the repetition of the same sound, usually a consonant, at the beginning of two or more adjacent words

antithesis: a rhetorical contrast achieved by the balanced or parallel arrangement of words, clauses, or sentences with a strong contrast in meaning

assonance: the repetition of the same vowel sounds in two or more adjacent words

asyndeton: the omission of conjunctions or customary connecting words

atmosphere: the mood pervading the literary work

cadence: a measured rhythmic sequence or flow of words in prose or poetry

connotation: the cluster of implicit or associated meanings of a word as distinguished from that word's denotative or specific meaning

diction: the deliberate choice of words

ellipsis: the omission of word(s) necessary for the grammatical structure of a sentence

emphatic word order:
- (i) **chiasmus**: a criss-cross arrangement usually resulting from the separation of two nouns and the adjectives that modify each
- (ii) **first and last word positions**: placing an important word at these emphatic positions in a line of poetry
- (iii) **framing**: a word placed out of its usual order and "framed" by a pair of related words to make the word stand out prominently
- (iv) **interlocking word order**: the words of one noun-adjective phrase alternating with those of another
- (v) **juxtaposition**: two words or phrases set side by side to intensify meaning
- (vi) **separation**: separating grammatically related words (e.g., noun—noun, noun—adjective) to produce a word picture of the meaning conveyed by the words

epic: a long narrative poem in elevated style, typically having as its subject a hero on whose exploits depends to some degree the fate of a nation or race

epic simile: a comparison extended beyond the obvious comparison by further details

epigram: a brief and pointed poem, usually ending with a surprising or witty turn of thought

figurative language: language that departs from the literal standard meaning in order to achieve a special effect, e.g., metaphor, personification, simile

genre: a literary form, e.g., epic, lyric, satire

hyperbole: an extravagant exaggeration of fact used to express strong feeling and not intended to be taken literally

imagery: the poetic technique of making mental pictures in such a way as to make the emotion or mood appeal vividly to the reader and to produce a clue to poetic intent
interjection: a sudden phrase or word that interrupts the grammatical progress of the sentence
irony: the use of words that convey a sense or attitude contrary to what is literally expressed; e.g., often ostensible praise or approval implies condemnation or contempt
metaphor: an indirect comparison whereby one thing is compared to another without the expressed indication of the point of similarity
mythological allusion: a brief reference to mythological details the writer assumes will be readily recognized by the reader instead of stating directly the myth or name of the person or thing
onomatopoeia or imitative harmony: the use of a word whose sound resembles the sound it describes
oxymoron: a rhetorical contrast achieved by putting together two contradictory terms
paradox: a statement that seems contradictory but that reveals a coherent truth
parallelism or balanced structure: the recurrence or repetition of a grammatical pattern
pathos: the creation of pity or sorrow in the reader
periodic sentence: a sentence designed to arouse interest and suspense by keeping the meaning unclear until the very end
personification: the description of an inanimate object or concept in terms of human qualities
rhetoric: the presentation of ideas in a persuasive manner, usually used for effectiveness in oratory or public speaking; for specific rhetoric devices, see anaphora, alliteration, etc.
rhetorical question: a question used for its persuasive effect and for which no answer is expected or for which the answer is self-evident; it is used to achieve rhetorical emphasis stronger than a direct statement
rhythm: the pattern of long and short syllables in each line of poetry
rhyme: the repetition of the same sound at the end of two or more words
satire: a literary form in which prevailing vices or follies are held up to humour and ridicule and evoke towards them attitudes of amusement, indignation, or contempt
simile: a stated comparison often indicated by a term such as *velut*, *similis*, or *qualis*. A simile extended to embellish, complete, or reinforce the narrative with a vivid picture, the details of which are not always relevant to the original point of comparison, is called an **epic simile**.
theme: the central or dominating idea of a literary work
tone: the attitude of the writer to the subject. The tone may be characterized, for example, as formal or informal, solemn or playful, satirical, serious, or ironic.
transferred epithet: the application of a significant modifier to a word other than the one to which it actually belongs
vivid particularization: a concrete or specified description, usually achieved by the use of proper nouns rich in connotations

SHORT BIOGRAPHIES OF LATIN AUTHORS QUOTED IN *MULTAS PER GENTES*

Caesar: General, Statesman, Orator, and Writer (c. 100 B.C. —44 B.C.)

Gaius Julius Caesar is probably better known to the student than any other person from the ancient world because of the month of July, which is named after him, and the popular play of Shakespeare, *Julius Caesar*. Born of noble parents, Caesar traced his descent from Ascanius (Iulus), the son of Aeneas. After a period of military service and rhetorical training in the east in his late teens, Caesar returned to Rome; he entered politics in his thirties and served, in order, as quaestor, aedile, praetor, and finally consul in 59 B.C. After his consulship, Caesar was made proconsul for Cisalpine Gaul and neighbouring Illyria. The nine years 58-50 B.C. were occupied in conquering Transalpine Gaul (modern France and Belgium) and two invasions of Britain. In 49, now a famous general himself, he brought his army illegally into Italy and launched a civil war against Pompey, whom he defeated the following year. Thereafter, Caesar ruled as dictator in Rome until he was assassinated in 44 B.C.

Caesar was the author of seven books of *Commentarii (De Bello Gallico)* on his campaigns in Gaul, Britain, and Germany and three books on the civil war *(De Bello Civili)*. Although both works were intended to justify his actions, Caesar was still able to provide an objective and dramatic account of his campaigns. His writings have been highly praised for their qualities of style—clarity, compression, absence of rhetoric, and purity of diction— which have made Caesar a model for Latin prose for generations of high-school students.

Cicero: Orator, Statesman, Philosopher, Letter Writer (106 B.C.—43 B.C.)

Marcus Tullius Cicero was born in Arpinum, southeast of Rome, of a family of equestrian rank. In Rome, he studied rhetoric and philosophy, the culminating subjects of Roman education. Beginning with his successful prosecution of the governor Verres in 70 B.C., Cicero used his success as a lawyer to advance politically through the various grades of public office to the consulship in 63 B.C. and governorship of Cilicia in 52 B.C. He was proscribed and killed by the second triumvirate in 43 B.C.

Besides being the greatest of Roman orators, Cicero was a prolific writer who left us forensic and political speeches, theoretical works on rhetoric and philosophy, and nearly 800 letters. Cicero is known for his periodic style with its orderly development of thought, balanced clauses, and rhetorical figures of speech. It is because of his voluminous literary works, especially his letters and speeches, that we know more about his life and his age than any other period of Roman history.

Curtius: Historian (first century A.D.)

Quintus Curtius Rufus' identity is subject to a great debate. He may have been a gladiator's son and the soldier and politician who rose from obscurity to a senatorial career under Tiberius (A.D. 14-37) and served as proconsul of Africa under Claudius in A.D. 53 where he probably died during his tenure.

He wrote in ten books the only history in Latin of Alexander the Great. The eight surviving books narrate Alexander's career from 333 B.C. to his death at Babylon in 323 B.C. Making reliable use of his sources and composing in a rhetorical and dramatic style reminiscent of Livy, Curtius, a moralist, wrote about Alexander's exploits with clarity and elegance. He can be counted on to provide his reader with a valuable, entertaining, and exciting historical source full of dramatic incidents and delightful character sketches.

Horace: Poet (65 B.C.—8 B.C.)

Quintus Horatius Flaccus was born in Venusia in southern Italy. His father, a freedman and tax-collector, amassed sufficient money to send his son to Rome and Athens for an excellent education which helped shape his attitudes for the rest of his life. While studying philosophy in Athens, Horace met Brutus, the assassin of Caesar, and later fought on his side as a military tribune at Philippi in 42 B.C. Returning to Rome under an amnesty, he found his farm confiscated. He therefore purchased the post of clerk in the treasury and began writing his *Satires* and *Epodes*, through which he became known in literary circles. In 38 B.C. he was introduced by the poet Vergil to Maecenas, close adviser of Octavian (later known as Augustus) and patron of literature. Horace's fortunes now turned for the better. He soon became a close friend of Maecenas and accompanied him on his diplomatic journey to Brundisium in 37 B.C. From Maecenas he received an estate in the Sabine hills which provided a refuge from the daily turmoil of Rome and enabled him, free from financial worries, to devote himself to his first love, poetry. Later, without losing imperial favour, Horace declined the emperor's offer of becoming his private secretary.

Among Horace's literary works are the *Satires*, *Ars Poetica*, and *Odes*. Amongst his earlier works, the *Satires* (published by 30 B.C.) humorously describe the poet's own life and his personal views on social and literary topics, as opposed to the political satire of his predecessor Lucilius. The *Ars Poetica*, an essay on literary criticism, is still studied at universities by students of English literature. Horace's poetical fame mainly rests with the *Odes* (Books I to III published in 23 B.C. and Book IV about 13 B.C.). In adapting the traditional Greek lyric metres to the Latin language the poet ranged from lighter themes of wine and women to serious topics such as philosophy, religion, and politics. It was Horace's method of expressing ideas and his mastery of sound, word, and rhythm that made him the most quotable poet of his time.

Livy: Historian (64 or 59 B.C.—A.D. 17 or 12)

Titus Livius, born at Patavium (Padua) in northern Italy, then called Cisalpine Gaul, went to Rome in about 31 B.C., and spent most of his life there. We know little about his family background, but we do know that he devoted his long life to writing a monumental history of Rome. His work apparently brought him into contact with Augustus, who encouraged a revival of interest in the origins and early history of the Roman people. A tombstone inscription found at Padua confirms his retirement to his native city and death there.

Livy's history, known as *Ab Urbe Condita*, contained 142 books (35 are still extant) describing the rise of Rome from its foundation down to 9 B.C. He aimed to instil in his fellow Romans a pride in their glorious past and likewise a belief in a glorious future under the reign of Augustus. His lively style included many poetic words, varied sentence structure, vivid details, moral episodes and rhetorical speeches. Livy's strength is not as a historical critic. He is often condemned for his careless use of annalistic sources and his inaccurate descriptions of battles and of geography. For instance, modern scholars have found it difficult to trace Hannibal's route over the Alps from Livy's dramatic, visual account of this event. Rather, his strength is as a historical writer describing events, moods, and characters in an instructive, patriotic manner.

Ovid: Poet (43 B.C.—A.D. 17)

Publius Ovidius Naso was born of an equestrian family at Sulmo, 145 km east of Rome. He studied rhetoric and law at Rome and philosophy at Athens. After holding minor official posts he abandoned public life for poetry and was soon recognized as the leading poet in Rome. In A.D. 8 he fell into disfavour with Augustus and was banished for some unknown reason to Tomis on the Black Sea, where he passed the remainder of his life.

Ovid's most important contribution to literature was his poem the *Metamorphoses* which describes transformations or changes in nature. It was Ovid's extraordinary power to isolate the significant moment in each scene or episode, such as the flight of Daedalus and Icarus, that influenced later writers and artists. The *Metamorphoses* became the standard source book on mythology.

Tacitus: Historian and Statesman (c. A.D. 56—c. A.D. 117)

Publius Cornelius Tacitus, born in Gaul or northern Italy, studied rhetoric in Rome, and soon became one of the best-known speakers of his time in the law courts and in the senate. At the age of twenty-two he married the daughter of Agricola, then consul and soon to be governor of Britain. Armed with this family link he soon held the high positions of state prosecutor, praetor, consul, and provincial governor.

Tacitus' literary works include the *Agricola* (A.D. 98), a biography of his father-in-law; the *Histories*, which describe the rule of the emperors from Galba to Domitian (A.D. 69-96); and the *Annals*, which narrate the rule of the Julio-Claudian emperors,

Tiberius, Gaius (Caligula), Claudius, and Nero from A.D. 14 to 68. Tacitus' historical writings display a moral purpose and keen insight into character and events. His gifts of "spotlighting" the action and of psychological insight are illustrated by his portrayal of the Roman attack on the Druid stronghold of Anglesey. His writing style is annalistic, dramatic, rhetorical, terse, epigrammatic, and sometimes ironical. His mastery of atmosphere, his noble style, his command of evidence, his accuracy, and his sense of history made Tacitus the premier Roman historian.

Vergil: Poet (70 B.C.—19 B.C.)

Publius Vergilius Maro, the most widely read of all Latin poets and one of the chief formative influences of Western civilization, was born of peasant stock near Mantua in northern Italy. He spent his childhood on his father's farm in the fertile Po river valley and grew to love the Italian country landscape. He was educated at Cremona, at Milan, and finally at Rome where he immersed himself in Greek literature and philosophy. After his family's property was confiscated by the triumvirs in 40 B.C., powerful friends secured for him an estate in Campania near Naples where Vergil could pursue his writing career and at his leisure could return to Rome to visit his friends, Maecenas and Augustus.

Vergil wrote three major works: the *Eclogues* (42-37 B.C.), pastoral poems modelled on the Sicilian Theocritus; the *Georgics* (37-30 B.C.), which describe crops, animals, beekeeping, and his deep love for rural Italy and its farmers; and the *Aeneid* (30-19 B.C.), an epic poem designed to glorify Rome and Augustus by means of the saga of the legendary hero, Aeneas, whom Augustus claimed as an ancestor. Vergil modelled his epic on Homer's *Odyssey* and *Iliad*: the first six books contain the wanderings of Aeneas and his Trojan band; the last six books describe the battles in Italy, in which Aeneas wins the right to settle there. The passages in this book pertain to the wandering hero's encounter with the Cyclops, Polyphemus, in Sicily and his journey through the underworld near Cumae. It is reported that on his deathbed Vergil ordered his executors to burn his manuscript because he considered it unfinished. But the emperor Augustus himself countermanded his instructions and preserved for posterity the poet's masterpiece. Vergil's greatness as a poet was recognized by the Roman people, who often listened to recitations of the *Aeneid* in the theatre, admitted his epic poem into Roman schools as textbooks, and even scribbled memorable lines from it on their walls as graffiti.

What qualities make Vergil's *Aeneid* relevant today two thousand years after his death? First, he is remembered for his technical skills: (1) an ability to make the sound of words echo the meaning; (2) a descriptive power enabling the reader to imagine and visualize the scene; (3) an ability to tell a well-structured story in an exciting way. Secondly, the poem expresses his interpretation of life and his thoughts on human character, the gods, and the afterlife, and the universal problem of how the frail, private, sensitive, vulnerable individual copes with the strong political, organizational, intellectual, impersonal, world of the state.

Vergil is described as tall, slender, and with a dark complexion. He suffered from ill health and he never married.

INTRODUCTION

For centuries, people of all ages have enjoyed stories about heroes and their travels and adventures in far-off lands. The ancient traveller or pioneer had to overcome many fears and obstacles on land and water in exploring previously unknown lands like Britain, Gaul, and India.

Resourcefulness was the operative word for the would-be traveller. Twenty-three hundred years ago there were no air-conditioned cars, no airplanes, no trains, and no all-weather highways. Roads were few and far between. Because travelling was so perilous, most people stayed at home. The main travellers were merchants and soldiers who went in large numbers for protection. Consequently, what we learn from the ancient writer about geography, peoples, customs, and travels often focuses on the accounts of generals as they invade new lands.

The selected Latin passages in this book are divided into four sections: Geography, Customs, and People; Ancient Sites; Travel by Land, Water, and Air; A Journey Through the Underworld.

Our guides are the historians Julius Caesar, Livy, Quintus Curtius, and Tacitus, and the poets Horace, Ovid, and Vergil. The paths of our journeys back in time include Aeneas's seven-year journey across the Mediterranean Sea and his passage through the underworld, Daedalus and Icarus' flight of fantasy, a Roman general's travel itinerary for Greece, Caesar's landing in Britain, Suetonius Paulinus' attack on the Druidic stronghold in Wales, Hannibal's crossing of the Alps, and Alexander the Great's boat journey down the Indus River in Pakistan.

In closing, you should be challenged to compare your own motives for travel with those heroes of the past who experienced the hardship of the elements in their quest to conquer, explore, and civilize. As we make travelling less arduous and time-consuming in our ever-shrinking global village, consider that the excitement of travel never leaves us. The experience of seeing something new and making our own observations will remain with us always.

PART I
GEOGRAPHY, CUSTOMS, AND PEOPLE

A relief from the palace at Persepolis. The relief shows Persian nobles bringing tribute to their king. Alexander probably met nobles who wore this type of hairstyle and clothing. Photo by Paul Whalen.

Desert region in modern-day Iran. The land in this picture is not unlike the Gedrosian desert that Alexander's army had to cross in 325 B.C. An account of Alexander's journey through the desert can be found on page 32 of this book. Photo by Paul Whalen.

The Geography of India

in illa plaga mundus statas temporum vices adeo
mutat, ut, cum alia fervore solis exaestuant, Indiam
nives obruant. terra lini ferax; inde plerisque sunt
vestes. libri arborum teneri haud secus quam chartae
litterarum notas capiunt. aves ad imitandum humanae
vocis sonum dociles sunt. elephantorum maior est vis
quam quos in Africa domitant, et viribus magnitudo
respondet. aurum flumina vehunt. gemmas margaritasque mare litoribus infundit.

    in interioribus Indiae silvae erant prope in immensum spatium diffusae et in eximiam altitudinem editis arboribus umbrosae. plerique rami instar ingentium stipitum flexi in humum, rursus qua se curvaverant erigebantur, adeo ut species esset non rami resurgentis, sed arboris ex sua radice generatae. caeli temperies salubris; quippe et vim solis umbrae levant et aquae large manant e fontibus. ceterum hic quoque serpentium magna vis erat, squamis fulgorem auri reddentibus. virus haud ullum magis noxium est; quippe et morsum praesens mors sequebatur donec ab incolis remedium oblatum est.

                Curtius, *Historiae Alexandri* VIII.ix.13-19; IX.i.9-12

The Hercynian Forest of Germany

Hercyniae silvae latitudo novem dierum iter expedito patet. neque quisquam est huius Germaniae qui se aut adisse ad initium eius silvae dicat, cum dierum iter LX processerit, aut quo ex loco oriatur, acceperit.

    multaque in ea genera ferarum nasci constat, quae reliquis in locis visa non sint. sunt uri magnitudine paulo infra elephantos, specie et colore et figura tauri. hos studiose foveis captos interficiunt. adulescentes, qui plurimos ex his interfecerunt, relatis in publicum cornibus, quae sint testimonio, magnam ferunt laudem. haec studiose conquisita ab labris argento circumcludunt atque in amplissimis epulis pro poculis utuntur.

                Caesar, *De Bello Gallico* VI.25-28

The Geography of India

Accompanying Alexander the Great on his march through Asia to India in 334-325 B.C. were historians, geographers, botanists, astronomers, and philosophers who collected information and specimens about nearly every aspect of these unknown lands, including their inhabitants, terrain, and flora and fauna.

---

plaga, ae, f   quarter, region
mundus, i, m   earth
statas...mutat   Tr. "so alters the regular changes of seasons"
fervor, oris, m   boiling heat
exaestuo, are   bake, swelter
nix, nivis, f   snow
obruo, ere   cover
linum, i, n   flax
ferax, acis + gen.   abounding in
plerisque   Tr. "for most of the inhabitants"
liber, libri, m   inner bark: from this use of the inner bark, "*liber*" came to mean book
tener, tenera, tenerum   soft
5 *haud...capiunt*   Tr. "takes written characters just as papyrus does"
docilis, e   easily taught (i.e., parrots)
domito, are   tame
respondeo, ere   correspond, match
margarita, ae, f   pearl
litus, oris, n   shore
10 *diffusus, a, um*   spread out
eximius, a, um   remarkable

editus, a, um   lofty, towering
arboribus   (i.e., banyan, an Indian fig-bearing tree whose branches send down aerial roots that develop into new trunks, producing a shady grove that could shelter fifty horsemen)
umbrosus, a, um   giving shade
ramus, i, m   branch
stipes, itis, m   trunk
qua   Tr. "from where"
erigebantur   Tr. "would shoot up straight"
species, ei, f   appearance
15 *radix, icis, f*   root
generatus, a, um   sprung
caeli temperies salubris   Tr. "the healthy temperature of the air"
quippe = *nam, enim*
levo, are   temper, alleviate, lessen
serpentium...vis   Tr. "number of serpents"
squama, ae, f   scale
fulgor, oris, m   gleam, glitter
virus, i, n   poison, venom
20 *morsus, i, m*   bite
praesens, entis   instant, immediate
donec   until

The Hercynian Forest of Germany

The Hercynian Forest was a huge wooded area extending from the Rhine River to the Carpathian Mountains in present-day Romania and Ukraine.

---

expedito   Tr. "for one travelling light"
pateo, ere   extend
huius Germaniae   (i.e., western Germany)
oriatur   it starts
accipio, ere, accepi   learn
5 *nascor, nasci*   be found
constat   it is established, well known
urus, i, m   aurochs or wild ox: the aurochs was hunted to extinction by about A.D. 1600

infra + acc.   smaller than
studiose   eagerly
fovea, ae, f   pit
10 *cornu, us, n*   horn: the horns were 80 cm long
conquisitus, a, um   collected
labrum, i, n   brim, rim
circumcludo, ere   surround, put round
amplus, a, um   magnificent, splendid
epula, ae, f   feast

The People of India

ingenia hominum, sicut ubique, apud illos locorum quoque situs format. corpora usque pedes carbaso velant, soleis pedes, capita linteis vinciunt, lapilli ex auribus pendent. capillum pectunt saepius quam tondent; mentum semper intonsum est, reliquam oris cutem ad speciem levitatis exaequant. regum luxuria, quam ipsi magnificentiam appellant, super omnium gentium vitia. rex aurea lectica margaritis circumpendentibus recubat; distincta sunt auro et purpura carbasa quae indutus est.

   unum agreste genus est, quod sapientes vocant. apud hos occupare fati diem pulchrum, et vivos se cremari iubent quibus aut segnis aetas aut incommoda valetudo est. illi siderum motus scite spectare dicuntur et futura praedicere. deos putant quidquid colere coeperunt, arbores maxime, quas violare capital est.

Curtius, Historiae Alexandri VIII.ix.20-35

The People of Germany

Germani multum consuetudine differunt. nam neque druides habent, qui rebus divinis praesint, neque sacrificiis student. deorum numero eos solos ducunt, quos cernunt et quorum aperte opibus iuvantur, Solem et Vulcanum et Lunam. vita omnis in venationibus atque in studiis rei militaris consistit.

   agri culturae non student, maiorque pars eorum victus in lacte, caseo, carne consistit. neque quisquam agri modum certum aut fines habet proprios; sed magistratus ac principes in annos singulos gentibus cognationibusque hominum, qui una coierunt, quantum et quo loco visum est agri attribuunt atque anno post alio transire cogunt. eius rei multas afferunt causas: ne, assidua consuetudine capti, studium belli gerendi agri cultura commutent; ne latos fines parare studeant, potentioresque humiliores possessionibus expellant; ne accuratius ad frigora atque aestus vitandos aedificent; ne qua oriatur pecuniae cupiditas, qua ex re factiones dissensionesque nascuntur; ut animi aequitate plebem contineant, cum suas quisque opes cum potentissimis aequari videat.

Caesar, De Bello Gallico VI.21-22

The People of India

Curtius describes the various classes of people in India.

---

ingenium, ii, n natural ability
situs, us, m arrangement, position
carbasus, i, f linen cloth
solea, ae, f sandal
linteum, i, n linen cloth (here, "turban")
lapillus, i, m precious stone, gem
capillus, i, m hair
pecto, ere comb
tondeo, ere trim
5 *mentum, i, n* chin
intonsus, a, um unshorn
cutis, is, f skin
ad speciam levitatis Tr. "so that it looks smooth"
exaequo, are shave close
vitium, ii, n vice
lectica, ae, f litter, sedan-chair
recubo, are lie back, recline
carbasa, orum, n linen clothes

10 *quae indutus est* Tr. "which he has put on"
agrestis, e uncivilized, uncouth
sapientes Tr. "wise men": Curtius may have read or heard something about Brahmans, members of the highest or priestly caste among the Hindus
fatum, i, n death
occupo, are lit., seize (here, "anticipate")
pulchrum (est) it is noble
cremo, are burn
quibus segnis aetas Tr. "whose time of life is past activity"
incommodus, a, um impaired
valetudo, inis, f health
sidus, eris, n star
scite skilfully
15 *futura* the wise men's prophecies dealt with weather, crops, and politics
capital, is, n a capital offence

The People of Germany

Caesar highlights the customs and traditions of the tribes living east of the Rhine River.

---

praesum, esse + dat. be in charge
studeo, ere + dat. pursue, be devoted to
duco, ere consider, reckon
cerno, ere see
opes, um, f resources, wealth
iuvo, are assist, benefit
5 *venatio, onis, f* hunting
studium, i, n pursuit
victus, us, m diet, nourishment
lac, lactis, n milk
caseus, i, m cheese
caro, carnis, f meat
modus, modi, m amount
fines, ium, f property
proprius, a, um one's own
10 *in annos singulos* every year
gentibus...hominum Tr. "to clans and groups of kinsmen"

coeo, ire, ii unite, combine
quantum + gen. as much as
attribuo, ere allot, assign
transeo, ire pass
affero, ferre allege, produce
assidua consuetudine: Tr. "by the continuous custom" (i.e., of living in one place)
15 *commuto, are* replace
paro, are acquire, obtain
humilis, e weak
accuratius, adv. more carefully
aestus, us, m heat
vito, are avoid (here, "keep out")
nascor, nasci originate, spring forth
19 *animi aequitate* with contentment
aequo, are make equal

The Druids

Druides a bello abesse consuerunt neque tributa una cum reliquis pendunt. militiae vacationem omniumque rerum habent immunitatem. tantis excitati praemiis et sua sponte multi in disciplinam conveniunt et a parentibus propinquisque mittuntur. magnum ibi numerum versuum ediscere dicuntur. itaque annos non nulli XX in disciplina permanent. neque fas esse existimant ea litteris mandare, cum in reliquis fere rebus, publicis privatisque rationibus, Graecis litteris utantur. id mihi duabus de causis instituisse videntur, quod neque in vulgum disciplinam efferri velint neque eos qui discunt litteris confisos minus memoriae studere.

   in primis hoc volunt persuadere, non interire animas, sed ab aliis post mortem transire ad alios; atque hoc maxime ad virtutem excitari putant, metu mortis neglecto. multa praeterea de sideribus atque eorum motu, de mundi ac terrarum magnitudine, de rerum natura, de deorum immortalium vi ac potestate disputant et iuventuti tradunt.

Caesar, De Bello Gallico VI.14

Human Sacrifices

natio est omnis Gallorum admodum dedita religionibus, atque ob eam causam qui sunt affecti gravioribus morbis, quique in proeliis periculisque versantur, aut pro victimis homines immolant aut se immolaturos vovent, administrisque ad ea sacrificia Druidibus utuntur; quod pro vita hominis nisi hominis vita reddatur, non posse deorum immortalium numen placari arbitrantur, publiceque eiusdem generis habent instituta sacrificia. alii immani magnitudine simulacra habent, quorum contexta viminibus membra vivis hominibus complent; quibus succensis circumventi flamma exanimantur homines. supplicia eorum, qui in furto aut in latrocinio aut aliqua noxia sint comprehensi, gratiora dis immortalibus esse arbitrantur; sed, cum eius generis copia defecit, etiam ad innocentium supplicia descendunt.

Caesar, De Bello Gallico VI.16

The Druids

Caesar outlines the duties and beliefs of the privileged, learned, priestly class of Celtic society, known as the Druids.

Druides, um, m Druids
tributum, i, n tax
una, adv. together
pendo, ere pay
militia, ae, f military service
vacatio, onis, f exemption
excito, are, avi, atus kindle
sua sponte of their own accord
disciplina, ae, f instruction, training
5 *propinquus, i, m* relative
edisco, ere learn by heart
fas, indeclinable adj. lawful, right
litterae, arum, f writing
mando, are commit, entrust
cum although
ratio, onis, f account
effero, efferre, extuli, elatus bring out
10 *Graecis litteris utantur* Tr. "they use the Greek alphabet"
confisus, a, um relying on
minus...studere pay less attention to
vulgus, i, m ordinary people
in primis especially
intereo, ire perish, die
15 *transeo, ire* pass over
sidus, eris, n heavenly body
mundus, i, m universe
vis, vis, f force
20 *iuventus, utis, f* youth
trado, ere instruct

Human Sacrifices

To the Celts, human sacrifice was simply a means by which their priests could communicate with the gods and thereby foretell and advise on future events. As several Roman writers have indicated, the Roman viewed human sacrifice with disgust although the Romans themselves came from a society that enjoyed as entertainment mass slaughter of gladiators and wild beasts in the amphitheatre.

admodum, adv. extremely
deditus, a, um devoted to
religio, onis, f religious observance
morbus, i, m disease
versor, ari be engaged
immolo, are sacrifice: human beings were stabbed in the back and the future foretold by their death-throes
5 *voveo, ere* vow
administer, tri, m officiator
utor, uti + abl. use
reddo, ere exchange
numen, inis, n power
placo, are propitiate, appease
institutus, a, um established
immanis, e monstrous, huge
simulacrum, i, n image: a figure resembling a human form
10 *contexo, ere, xui, textus* weave, construct
vimen, inis, n twig
membrum, i, n limb
vivus, a, um living
succendo, ere, i, ensus set on fire
exanimo, are kill
supplicium, ii, n punishment
furtum, i, n theft
latrocinum, i, n armed robbery
noxia, ae, f crime
dis = deis
arbitror, ari believe
15 *deficio, ere, feci* be lacking

The Druid Stronghold of Anglesey

igitur Suetonius Monam insulam, incolis validam et receptaculum perfugarum, adgredi parat; navesque fabricatur plano alveo adversus breve et incertum. sic pedes; equites vado secuti aut altiores inter undas adnantes equis tramisere. stabat pro litore diversa acies, densa armis virisque, intercursantibus feminis; in modum Furiarum veste ferali, crinibus deiectis faces praeferebant; Druidaeque circum, preces diras sublatis ad caelum manibus fundentes, novitate aspectus ita perculere milites ut quasi haerentibus membris immobile corpus vulneribus praeberent. dein cohortationibus ducis et se ipsi stimulantes ne muliebre et fanaticum agmen pavescerent, inferunt signa sternuntque obvios et igni suo involvunt. praesidium posthac impositum victis excisique luci saevis superstitionibus sacri. nam Druidae cruore captivo adolere aras et hominum fibris consulere deos fas habebant.

                    Tacitus, *Annals* XIV. 29-30

The Druid Stronghold of Anglesey

In A.D. 61, the Roman governor of Britain, Suetonius Paulinus, attacked the Isle of Anglesey off the coast of what is now Wales. From the evidence of various objects (chariots, ornaments, a Druid slave-chain with five neck rings) found on the island, it seems clear that Anglesey was a Druid cult centre. The Druids were the leaders of resistance to Roman rule in Britain and Gaul. It was probably this fact more than their barbarous religious practice of human sacrifice that prompted strong measures like the ones described in this passage.

Mona, ae, f Mona, now called Anglesey, is a large island off the coast of Wales
incola, ae, m inhabitant
validus, a, um strong, powerful
receptaculum, i, n a place of refuge, retreat
perfuga, ae, m deserter
adgredior, adgredi attack
fabricor, ari build, construct
planus, a, um flat
alveus, i, m hull, bottom
adversus + acc. against
breve et incertum (maris) Tr. "shallow and uncertain depth of the sea"
pedes, itis, m infantry
eques, itis, m horseman
vadum, i, n shallows
secuti (sunt)
5 *adno, are* swim beside
tramisere = tramiserunt crossed
pro + abl. on the edge of, on
litus, oris, n shore
diversus, a, um hostile, of the enemy
acies, ei, f battleline
intercurso, are run among
feralis, e funereal
crinis, is, m hair
deiectus, a, um loose, dishevelled
fax, facis, f torch
praefero, ferre display, brandish
circum, adv. all around
prex, precis, f prayer
dirus, a, um awful, ominous, dreadful
sublatus, a, um held up, raised
novitas, atis, f strangeness
aspectus, us, m sight, appearance
10 *perculere = perculerunt*
percello, ere, perculi strike, scare, dispirit
haerentibus membris Tr. "with paralyzed limbs"
immobilis, e motionless
praebeo, ere offer, submit
cohortatio, onis, f encouragement, exhorting
dux, ducis, m general
stimulo, are urge, goad
muliebris, e female
fanaticus, a, um frenzied, hysterical
agmen, inis, n band
pavesco, ere begin to fear or dread
infero, inferre carry forward
signum, i, n standard
sterno, ere cut down
obvius, a, um in their way
igni suo involvunt Tr. "envelop in fire from their own torches"
praesidium, i, n garrison
posthac afterwards
15 *excido, ere, excidi, excisus* cut down
lucus, i, m grove; a sacred thicket of trees with a clearing in it for Celtic ritual
superstitiones, ium, f. pl. superstitious rites
cruor, oris, m blood
adoleo, ere make offerings at
fibrae, arum, f entrails
fas habebant Tr. "thought it right"

Achaemenides and Polyphemus

I ACHAEMENIDES TELLS HIS STORY

"hic me, dum trepidi crudelia limina linquunt,
immemores socii vasto Cyclopis in antro
deseruere. domus sanie dapibusque cruentis,
intus opaca, ingens. ipse arduus, altaque pulsat
sidera (di, talem terris avertite pestem!) 5
nec visu facilis nec dictu affabilis ulli.
visceribus miserorum et sanguine vescitur atro.
vidi egomet duo de numero cum corpora nostro
prensa manu magna medio resupinus in antro
frangeret ad saxum, sanieque aspersa natarent 10
limina; vidi atro cum membra fluentia tabo
manderet et tepidi tremerent sub dentibus artus—
haud impune quidem, nec talia passus Ulixes,
oblitusve sui est Ithacus discrimine tanto.
nam simul expletus dapibus vinoque sepultus 15
cervicem inflexam posuit, iacuitque per antrum
immensus, saniem eructans et frusta cruento
per somnum commixta mero, nos magna precati
numina sortitique vices una undique circum
fundimur, et telo lumen terebramus acuto 20
ingens quod torva solum sub fronte latebat,
Argolici clipei aut Phoebeae lampadis instar,
et tandem laeti sociorum ulciscimur umbras.
sed fugite, o miseri, fugite atque ab litore funem
rumpite! 25
nam qualis quantusque cavo Polyphemus in antro
lanigeras claudit pecudes atque ubera pressat,
centum alii curva haec habitant ad litora vulgo
infandi Cyclopes et altis montibus errant.
tertia iam lunae se cornua lumine complent 30
cum vitam in silvis inter deserta ferarum
lustra domosque traho, vastosque ab rupe Cyclopas
prospicio sonitumque pedum vocemque tremesco.
omnia collustrans hanc primum ad litora classem
conspexi venientem. huic me, quaecumque fuisset, 35
addixi: satis est gentem effugisse nefandam.
vos animam hanc potius quocumque absumite leto."

Vergil, *Aeneid* III.616-654

I Achaemenides Tells His Story

In their Odyssean wanderings, Aeneas and his band of followers travel along the coast of Sicily, enter a harbour beneath Mount Aetna, and meet Achaemenides, an emaciated Greek castaway and Ithican companion of Ulysses appealing for help.

---

limen, inis, n threshold, entrance
linquo, ere leave
Cyclops, opis, m one of a race of savage one-eyed giants
antrum, i, n cave
sanies, ei, f blood
daps, dapis, f feast
cruentus, a, um bloody
intus within, on the inside
opacus, a, um shady, shadowy
arduus, a, um towering
5 *pestis, is, f* plague
nec visu...ulli Tr. "not easy to look at nor able to be spoken to by anyone"
viscera, um, n entrails
vescor, vesci feed on
ater, atra, atrum black
egomet I, myself, with my own eyes
prensus, a, um lit., snatched up (here, "scooped up")
resupinus, a, um lying back, reclining
10 *aspersus, a, um* spattered
membrum, i, n limb
tabum, i, n gore
mando, ere chew, munch
artus, uum, m limbs
impunis, e unpunished
oblitus, a, um forgetful
discrimen, inis, n crisis, danger
15 *expletus, a, um* gorged
vino sepultus lit., buried in wine (here, "dead-drunk")
cervix, icis, f neck
inflexus, a, um drooping, bent
eructo, are belch forth
frustum, i, n morsel, bit, fragment
merum, i, n wine

numen, inis, n god
sortiti vices Tr. "having drawn lots for our tasks"
20 *lumen, inis, n* eye (lit., light)
terebro, are bore out
acutus, a, um sharp
torvus, a, um fierce
frons, frontis, m forehead
Argolicus, a, um Greek
clipeum, i, n shield
Phoebeae lampadis instar Tr. "like the lamp of Phoebus (i.e., the sun)"
ulciscor, i avenge
funis, is, m rope
25 *rumpo, ere* break: unfinished line here and at line 661 are among indications of the Aeneid's incomplete revision
laniger, gera, gerum woolly
claudo, ere pen
pecudes, um, f flock
ubera pressat Tr. "milks"
vulgo, adv. everywhere, up and down
29 *infandus, a, um* accursed, unspeakable
lustrum, i, n haunt
rupes, is, f rock
prospicio, ere look out, watch
tremesco, ere tremble
collustro, are survey
34 *classis, is, f* fleet
addico, ere, xi assign
nefandus, a, um unspeakable
potius rather
quicumque, quaecumque, quodcumque whatever
absumo, ere take away
letum, i, n death

II THE TROJANS ESCAPE FROM THE CYCLOPES

vix ea fatus erat, summo cum monte videmus
ipsum inter pecudes vasta se mole moventem
pastorem Polyphemum et litora nota petentem,
monstrum horrendum, informe, ingens, cui lumen
ademptum. 5
trunca manum pinus regit et vestigia firmat;
lanigerae comitantur oves; ea sola voluptas
solamenque mali.
postquam altos tetigit fluctus et ad aequora venit,
luminis effossi fluidum lavit inde cruorem 10
dentibus infrendens gemitu, graditurque per aequor
iam medium, necdum fluctus latera ardua tinxit.
nos procul inde fugam trepidi celerare, recepto
supplice sic merito tacitique incidere funem,
vertimus et proni certantibus aequora remis. 15
sensit, et ad sonitum vocis vestigia torsit.
verum ubi nulla datur dextra adfectare potestas
nec potis Ionios fluctus aequare sequendo,
clamorem immensum tollit, quo pontus et omnes
contremuere undae, penitusque exterrita tellus 20
Italiae, curvisque immugiit Aetna cavernis.
at genus e silvis Cyclopum et montibus altis
excitum ruit ad portus et litora complent.
cernimus adstantes nequiquam lumine torvo
Aetnaeos fratres, caelo capita alta ferentes, 25
concilium horrendum: quales cum vertice celso
aeriae quercus aut coniferae cyparissi
constiterunt, silva alta Iovis lucusve Dianae.
praecipites metus acer agit quocumque rudentes
excutere et ventis intendere vela secundis. 30

Vergil, *Aeneid* III.655-683

II The Trojans Escape from the Cyclopes

moles, is, f bulk, frame
horrendus, a, um dreadful, horrible
informis, e misshapen, shapeless
4 *lumen* Tr. "eye and sight"
ademptus, a, um put out
trunca pinus Tr. "trunk of a pine tree"
rego, ere guide
vestigium, ii, n footstep
firmo, are steady, support
commitor, ari accompany
ovis, is, f sheep
voluptas, atis, f pleasure
solamen, inis, n solace, comfort
tango, ere, tetigi touch
fluctus, us, m wave
aequor, is, n sea
10 *effossus, a, um* dug out, gouged out
fluidus, a, um flowing, trickling
lavo, ere, lavi wash
inde from it (*i.e.*, the water from the sea)
cruor, is, m blood
infrendo, ere grind, gnash
gemitus, us, m groaning, sighing
grador, gradi stride, wade
latus, eris, n side, flank
tingo, ere, tinxi wet
trepidus, a, um frightened, alarmed
celerare, historic infin. hasten
supplex, icis, m a suppliant
incidere, historic infin. cut
15 *pronus, a, um* bent over, leaning forward
certo, are strive, strain
aequora, um, n. pl. Tr. "surface of the sea"
remus, i, m oar
torqueo, ere, torsi turn quickly
verum but

adfecto, are grasp, clutch
potestas, atis, f power
aequo, are match, keep up with
pontus, i, m sea
20 *contremo, ere, ui* tremble, shudder
penitus deep within (*i.e.*, far inland)
curvus, a, um winding
immugio, ire, ii rumble, bellow
excitus, a, um roused
compleo, ere crowd, throng
cerno, ere see
nequiquam foiled, powerless
torvus, a, um grim, glaring, fierce
25 *Aetnaeus, a, um* of Aetna
concilium, ii, n gathering, group
qualis, e just as
vertex, icis, m top, summit
celsus, a, um lofty
aerius, a, um reaching high into the air, lofty
quercus, us, f oak tree
conifer, fera, ferum cone-bearing
lucus, i, m grove, woods: Diana the huntress was associated with woods and when identified as Hecate of the underworld was connected with cypresses, the trees of death
praeceps, praecipitis headlong
metus, us, m fear
quocumque wherever, in whatever direction
rudentes excutere Tr. "to slacken the sheets" (*i.e.*, let out the sails)
30 *ventus, i, m* wind
intendo, ere stretch out, unfurl
velum, i, n sail
secundus, a, um favourable

PART I: GEOGRAPHY, CUSTOMS, AND PEOPLE

Initial Questions

The Geography of India
1. Does Curtius hint at a possible reason for Alexander's invasion of India? Explain your answer.
2. What method of measurement does Curtius use to describe the size of a strange tree of India?
3. What indications in the passage suggest that Curtius was more interested in providing the reader with an exaggerated, entertaining description than in giving an accurate description of India?

The Hercynian Forest of Germany
1. What method of measurement does Caesar use to describe the extent of the Hercynian forest?
2. How does Caesar distinguish the urus from the bull?
3. Why did the Germans especially hunt the urus?

The People of India
1. What Latin words and phrases depict the wealthy Indians?
2. Is Curtius just describing or is he making an editorial comment when he uses the words *agrestis* and *horridus* to describe the wise men?

The People of Germany
1. (a) Why are the German tribesmen not allowed to own property?
   (b) Why do you think the Germans had no sense of ownership in the way that the Romans did or we do today?
2. Why didn't the Germans have a religious hierarchy similar to that of the Gauls or Indians? Does this mean that they were more primitive?

The Druids
1. What privileges did the Druids have that made their lives attractive for a would-be priest?
2. Why didn't the Druids commit their doctrines to writing?
3. What are the religious beliefs of Druids?

Human Sacrifices
1. Why did the Gauls have human sacrifices? Why was this practice considered abhorrent by the Romans?

The Druid Stronghold of Anglesey
1. What words does Tacitus use to make his description of the soldiers' crossing vivid and cinematic?
2. How does Tacitus describe the presence of the Druids and their initial effect on the Roman soldiers?
3. How does Tacitus convey the speed and efficiency of the Roman attack?
4. In view of Tacitus' statement at the beginning of this passage and the actions taken by Suetonius after the fighting ended, why do you think he travelled across unconquered territory to make this attack?

5. After rereading the passage, do you feel disgust, amusement, or sympathy for the enemy or for the Roman soldiers?
6. What was Tacitus' purpose in writing this narrative? Was he trying to present the facts and/or to entertain? or neither of these?

I Achaemenides Tells His Story
1. Describe the heightened tone and sustained hyperbole of the description of Polyphemus, who is portrayed as a cruel, revolting, inhuman, yet pathetic creature.

II The Trojans Escape from the Cyclopes
1. How does Vergil make the sound and movement of lines 1 to 4 match the sense?
2. Lines 23 to 27 are judged to be one of the most striking passages of visual imagery in the *Aeneid*. Suggest why.
3. Pick out some examples from sections I-II to show how Vergil uses simile, alliteration, assonance, asyndeton, pathos, emphatic word order, and imagery to reflect the tone of mystery, adventure, and the supernatural.

Discussion Questions
1. The aurochs had been hunted to extinction by about A.D. 1600. What are some of the causes for the extinction of species today? What are some conservation methods that are helping to stem the tide of extinction?
2. Is there any similarity between Curtius' description of the costume of the male Indian and that of the present-day Indian? Yes? No?
3. How similar or different are the native peoples, religious beliefs, and customs described by Caesar, Curtius, and Tacitus? Which account of the people did you like best? Why?
4. Do the authors in this section describe any problems that might face people planning to travel?
5. What do you think was the impact on Aeneas of his grim travel experiences with the Cyclopes?
6. What are the differences of attitude, intention, and style of Caesar, Curtius, and Tacitus?
7. How does the historian's approach in describing travel differ from that of the poet who writes a myth? How do both types of writer capture the interest of the reader?
8. In describing the Germans, was it Caesar's intention to draw a contrast between the luxurious, pleasure-loving Roman of his day and the primitive "savage" east of the Rhine?
9. Reread the passages in this section and determine whether our writers are like tourists who are fascinated by the mystique of visiting strange lands.

Further Readings
The geography and customs of the native people of Britain are described by Caesar and Tacitus: Caesar, *De Bello Gallico* V.12-14; Tacitus, *Agricola* 10-12.

Caesar describes the social structure of the Gauls: Caesar, *De Bello Gallico* VI.13-15.

Tacitus' monograph, *Germania*, is a study of the customs and character of the German tribes; in it Tacitus contrasts the virtues of the primitive German with the degenerate Roman of his day.

The Trojans land on the Strophades Islands in the Ionian Sea, kill some cattle for a meal, and are attacked by the insatiably hungry Harpies who pollute their food with their filth and smell: Vergil, *Aeneid* III. 209-277.

Juvenal satirizes the cannibalism of the Egyptians: Juvenal, *Satires* XV.33-131.

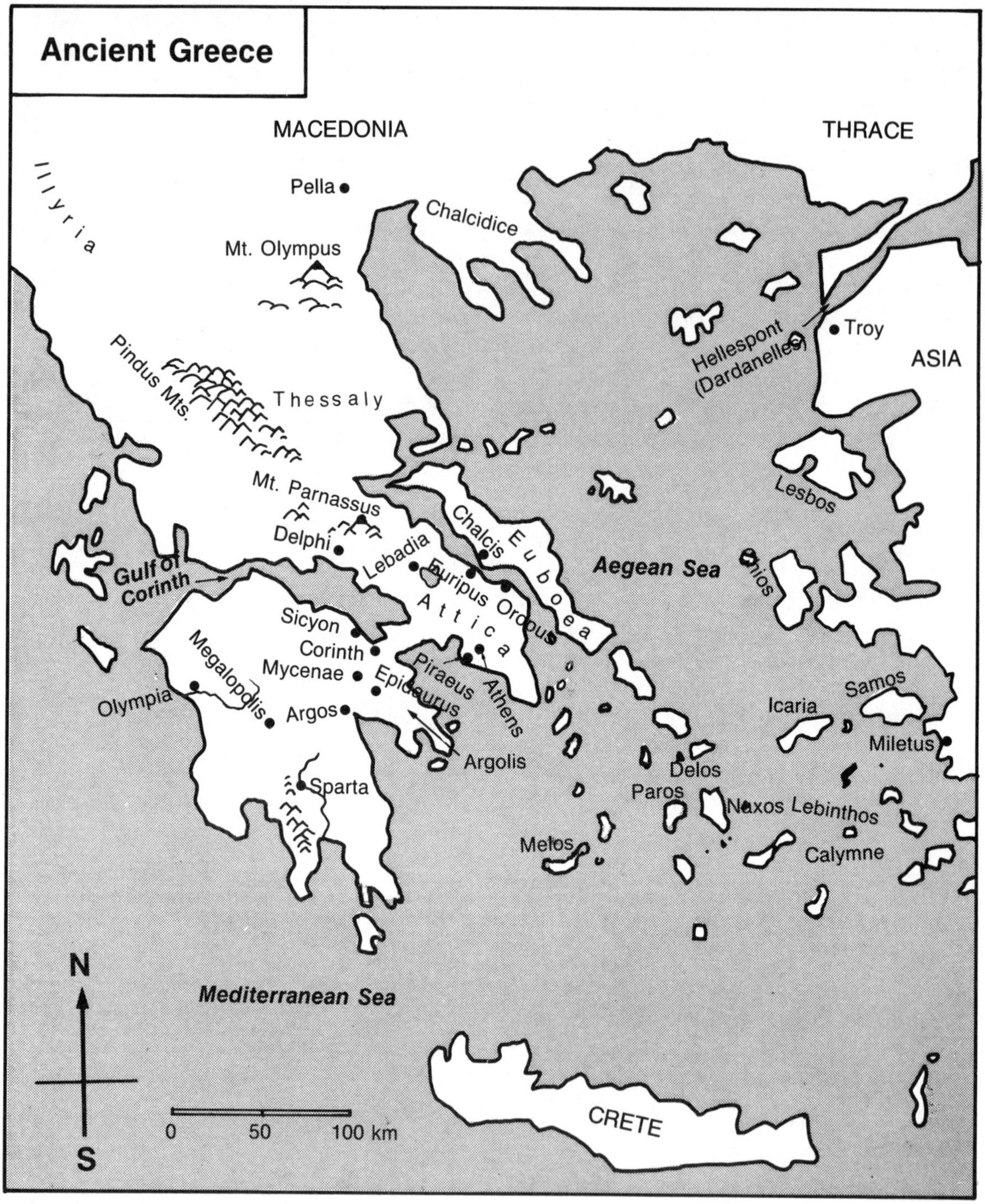
Ancient Greece
MACEDONIA
THRACE
Illyria
Pella
Chalcidice
Mt. Olympus
Troy
Hellespont
(Dardanelles)
ASIA
Pindus Mts.
Thessaly
Lesbos
Mt. Parnassus
Chalcis
Euboea
Delphi
Lebadia
Aegean Sea
Chios
Gulf of Corinth
Euripus
Oropus
Attica
Sicyon
Corinth
Megalopolis
Mycenae
Piraeus
Epidaurus
Athens
Samos
Icaria
Olympia
Argos
Miletus
Argolis
Delos
Sparta
Paros
Naxos
Lebinthos
Melos
Calymne
N
S
Mediterranean Sea
0
50
100 km
CRETE

PART II
ANCIENT SITES

The Hanging Gardens of Babylon, c. 600 B.C.*

An artist's conception of what the Hanging Gardens of Babylon might have looked like

Total area of the gardens: 31 m × 31 m

Height of supporting archways: 24 m

Height of the gardens: The lowest terrace was at the level of the top of the archways, i.e., 24 m above the ground. Each succeeding terrace was about 3 m higher, until the topmost terrace was about 40 m above ground level.

Area of each terrace: Assuming that there were half a dozen terraces (no one knows for sure how many there were), 30 m × 5 m

* NOTE: For an excerpt on The Hanging Gardens of Babylon taken from Curtius' *Historiae Alexandri*, see page 18 of this text.

The Hanging Gardens of Babylon*

ipsius urbis pulchritudo ac vetustas non regis modo, sed etiam omnium oculos in se haud immerito convertit. arcem ambitu XX stadia complexam habent. XXX pedes in terram turrium fundamenta demissa sunt, ad LXXX summum munimenti fastigium pervenit. super arcem, vulgatum Graecorum fabulis miraculum, pensiles horti sunt, summam murorum altitudinem aequantes multarumque arborum umbra et proceritate amoeni. saxo pilae, quae totum onus sustinent, instructae sunt, super pilas lapide quadrato solum stratum est patiens terrae, quam altam iniciunt, et humoris, quo rigant terras. adeo validas arbores sustinet moles, ut stipites earum VIII cubitorum spatium crassitudine aequent, in L pedum altitudinem emineant frugiferaeque sint, ut si terra sua alerentur. et cum vetustas non opera solum manu facta, sed etiam ipsam naturam paulatim exedendo perimat, haec moles, quae tot arborum radicibus premitur tantique nemoris pondere onerata est, inviolata durat; quippe XX pedes lati parietes sustinent, XI pedum intervallo distantes, ut procul visentibus silvae montibus suis imminere videantur. Syriae regem Babylone regnantem hoc opus esse molitum memoriae proditum est, amore coniugis victum, quae desiderio nemorum silvarumque in campestribus locis virum compulit amoenitatem naturae genere huius operis imitari.

diutius in hac urbe quam usquam constitit rex, nec alio loco disciplinae militari magis nocuit. nihil urbis eius corruptius moribus, nihil ad irritandas illiciendasque immodicas cupiditates instructius.

Curtius, *Historiae Alexandri* V.i.24-36

*NOTE: For an artist's conception of the Hanging Gardens of Babylon see page 17.

The Hanging Gardens of Babylon

Babylon, located on the Euphrates River not far from where the Iraqi capital of Baghdad now stands, was the site of the "Hanging Gardens," one of the seven wonders of the ancient world. To remind his young bride of her mountainous homeland, King Nebuchadnezzar (reigned c. 605-563 B.C.) had built terraced roof gardens on brick archways 24 m high. The gardens, which were lined with lead and pitch to keep the water in, towered to a height of 40 m above ground level. Today no trace is left of what Alexander viewed with amazement in 331 B.C.

---

vetustas, atis, f old age
ambitus, us, m circuit
stadium, ii, n a stade: a distance of about 186 m
complexus, a, um enclosed, surrounded
turris, is, f tower
fundamentum, i, n foundation
demitto, ere, misi, missus sink
5 *summum, i, n* top
munimentum, i, n fortification
fastigium, ii, n highest part
super + acc. on top of, upon
vulgatus, a, um celebrated
miraculum, i, n wonder
pensilis, e hanging
umbra, ae, f shade
proceritas, atis, f height
amoenus, a, um charming
saxo pilae Tr. "columns of stone"
onus, eris, n load, weight
10 *instruo, ere, xi, instructus* set up
quadratus, a, um square
solum, i, n foundation, floor
stratus, a, um made level
patiens, patientis capable of, bearing
altam Tr. "to a great depth"
humor, oris, m water: the rooftop garden was irrigated (*rigant*) by a chain of water buckets moving up through a tower to the upper level while slaves down below endlessly worked on a treadmill placed over a cistern holding river water
validus, a, um strong
moles, is, f massive structure

stipes, itis, m trunk
cubitum, i, n cubit: an ancient measure of length, about 50 cm
spatium, ii, n measure
crassitudo, inis, f thickness
15 *emineo, ere* tower, stand out
frugifer, era, erum fruit-bearing
alo, ere grow
cum although
exedo, ere eat away
perimo, ere destroy
radix, icis, f root
nemus, oris, n grove
pondus, eris, n weight
onero, are, avi, atus load
inviolatus, a, um undamaged
duro, are endure
quippe = nam, enim
20 *XX...parietes* Tr. "a substructure of walls 6 m thick"
silvae...imminere Tr. "woods overhanging their native mountains"
molior, iri, itus sum undertake
memoriae proditum est Tr. "there is a tradition"
desiderium, ii, n longing
25 *campester, tris, tre* flat: the area around Babylon was almost treeless
amoenitas, atis, f loveliness, pleasantness
genere huius operis = huius generis opere
irrito, are arouse, excite, stimulate
illicio, ere attract
30 *immodicus, a, um* dissolute, unbridled
cupiditas, atis, f passion
instructius more prepared, more planned

A Roman General Visits the Sites of Greece

Paulus initio autumni ad circumeundam Graeciam visendaque, quae nobilitata fama maiora auribus accepta sunt quam oculis noscuntur, uti statuit. cum haud magno comitatu per Thessaliam Delphos petit, inclutum oraculum. ubi sacrificio Apollini facto inchoatas in vestibulo columnas, quibus imposituri statuas regis Persei fuerant, suis statuis victor destinavit. Lebadiae quoque templum Iovis Trophonii adit; ibi cum vidisset os specus, per quod oraculo utentes sciscitatum deos descendunt, sacrificio Iovi Hercynnaeque facto, quorum ibi templum est. Chalcidem ad spectaculum Euripi Euboeaque, tantae insulae, ponte continenti iunctae descendit. a Chalcide Aulidem traicit, trium milium spatio distantem, portum inclutum statione quondam mille navium Agamemnoniae classis. inde Oropum Atticae ventum est, ubi pro deo vates antiquus colitur templumque vetustum est fontibus rivisque circa amoenum; Athenas inde, plenas quidem et ipsas vetustae famae, multa tamen visenda habentis, arcem, portus, muros Piraeum urbi iungentis, navalia, monumenta magnorum imperatorum, simulacra deorum hominumque, omni genere et materiae et artium insignia.

   sacrificio Minervae, praesidi arcis, in urbe facto profectus Corinthum altero die pervenit. urbs erat tunc praeclara ante excidium; arx intra moenia in immanem altitudinem edita, scatens fontibus; Isthmus duo maria occasu et ortu solis finitima artis faucibus dirimens. Sicyonem inde et Argos, nobiles urbes, adit; inde haud parem opibus Epidaurum, sed inclutam Aesculapi nobili templo, quod quinque milibus passuum ab urbe distans nunc vestigiis revolsorum donorum, tum donis dives erat, quae remediorum salutarium aegri mercedem sacraverant deo. inde Lacedaemonem adit, non operum magnificentia, sed disciplina institutisque memorabilem; unde per Megalopolim Olympiam ascendit. ubi et alia quidem spectanda ei visa; Iovem velut praesentem intuens motus animo est. itaque haud secus, quam si in Capitolio immolaturus esset, sacrificium amplius solito apparari iussit.

                  Livy, *Ab Urbe Condita* XLV.27-28

A Roman General Visits the Sites of Greece

In 167 B.C., after conquering Macedonia, the victorious Roman commander Aemilius Paulus decided to visit the famous sites of Greece. His tour ended at Olympia, the site of an ancient wonder of the world, Phidias's colossal statue of Zeus, 13 m high, resplendent with ivory for the flesh and gold sheeting for the drapery.

---

circumeo, ire travel around
nobilitatus, a, um made famous
fama, ae, f reputation
auribus Tr. "by hearsay"
oculis Tr. "when seen in person"
statuo, ere, ui decide
comitatus, us, m retinue, escort
5 *inclutus, a, um* renowned, famous
inchoatus, a, um unfinished
imposituri...fuerant Tr. "they had intended to place"
Perseius the last king of Macedonia
destino, are, avi reserve, choose
Lebadia, ae, f a Boeotian city famous for the oracle of Zeus (Jupiter) Trophonius
specus, us, m cave
10 *sciscitatum* Tr. "to put their questions"
Euripus, i, m the narrowest part of the strait between Boeotia and the island of Euboea, which is only 37 m wide and was considered a marvel of nature
continens, entis, f mainland
traicio, ere cross over
15 *statio, onis, f* anchorage
Agamemnon, onis, m King of Mycenae and leader of the Greek forces in the Trojan War
classis, is, f fleet
vates, is, m prophet: Amphiaraus, a Greek seer; those who sought the prophet's advice had to sacrifice a ram, sleep on the fleece in the *stoa*, and wait for a revelation in a dream; the Romans used this site as a health spa because of its healing spring waters and its natural beauty

vetustus, a, um ancient
rivus, i, m stream
amoenus, a, um pleasant
20 *arx, arcis, f* citadel (*i.e.*, the Acropolis)
navalia, ium, n. pl. shipyards
simulacrum, i, n statue
insignis, e outstanding, notable
praeses, idis, f presiding guardian
25 *praeclarus, a, um* famous, distinguished
ante excidium before destruction: Corinth was destroyed in 146 B.C. by the Roman general Mummius
editus, a, um elevated, rising up
scateo, ere gush forth with
fons, fontis, m spring
occasu et ortu solis Tr. "to the east and to the west"
finitimus, a, um + dat. neighbouring
artus, a, um narrow
fauces, ium, f passage
30 *dirimo, ere* separate
vestigia, ium, n. pl. traces
revolsus, a, um stripped, torn away
remediorum salutarium Tr. "for his health-giving remedies"
merces, edis, f payment
sacro, are, avi consecrate
35 *Lacedaemon, onis, f* Sparta
opus, eris, n public work
institutum, i, n institution
intueor, i observe
haud secus quam si just as if
40 *immolo, are, avi, atus* sacrifice
amplius apparari solito Tr. "to be prepared on a more lavish scale than usual": at each Olympic festival 100 oxen were sacrificed to Zeus

PART II: ANCIENT SITES

Initial Questions

The Hanging Gardens of Babylon
1. Why did a Babylonian king build the "Hanging Gardens"?
2. Does Curtius' description of the "Hanging Gardens" suggest terraces similar to huge modern window-boxes, filled with overhanging greenery? Use the diagram on page 17 to help you arrive at the answer.
3. What indications does the reader have that Curtius frowned on Alexander's lengthy stay in Babylon?

A Roman General Visits the Sites of Greece
1. Explain the meaning of "*quae nobilitata...noscuntur*" (ll. 2-3).
2. What were Paulus' motives for visiting each site?
3. Which sites on the general's travel itinerary are still visited today? Why are some sites omitted today?
4. With the exception of his visit to Olympia, Paulus' reactions to what he sees and observes are not recorded by Livy. Why not?
5. Would the reader have reacted in the same way as Paulus did to Phidias' statue of Zeus at Olympia?
6. What comments tell us that Livy was writing some time after this tour?
7. Trace Paulus' route on the map on page 16.

Discussion Questions

1. Does Paulus' choice of places to visit reflect the interests of the vast majority of tourists who came after him?
2. Should nations rebuild famous sites such as the Hanging Gardens of Babylon, Olympia, and the Acropolis? What are the pros and cons?

Further Readings

Alexander visits the site of the oracle of Jupiter Hammon in the Libyan desert: Curtius, *Historiae Alexandri* IV.7.
Evander conducts Aeneas on a tour of the ancient site of Rome: Vergil, *Aeneid* VIII, 280-369.

PART III
TRAVEL BY LAND, WATER, AND AIR

The Route of Alexander's Journey

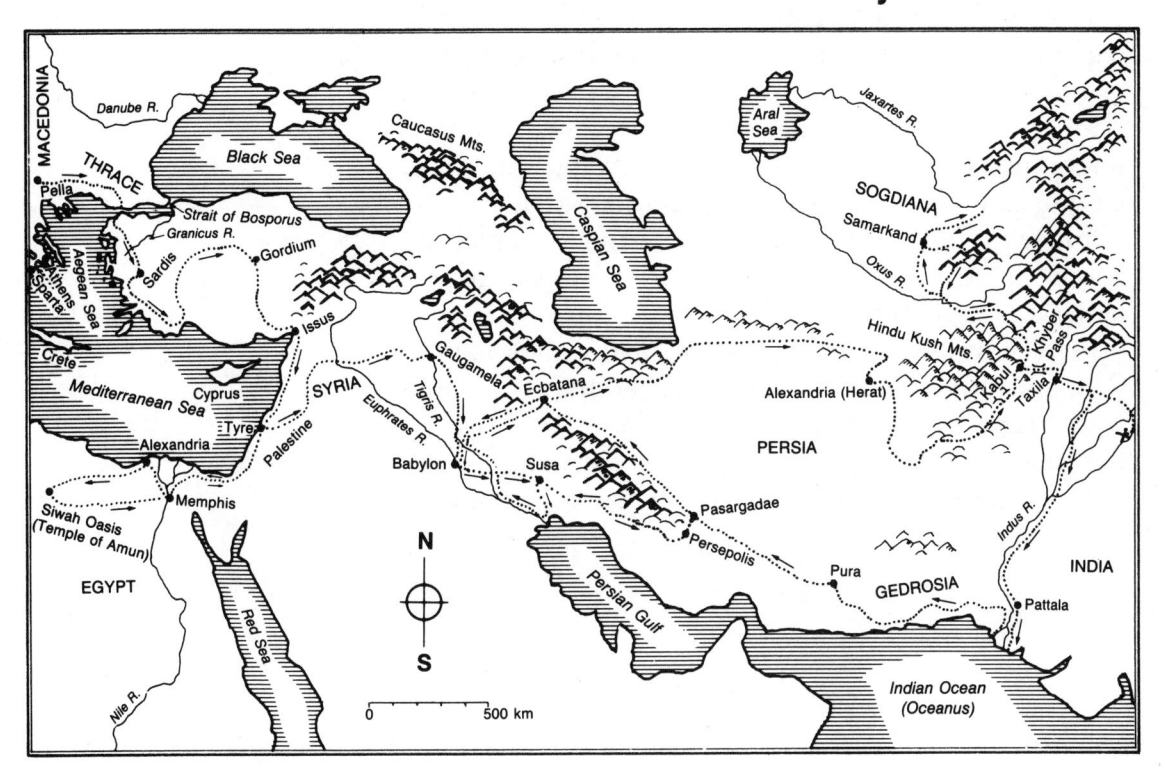

A Roman Governor Tours His Province

itinerum laborem, iudices, accipite quam facilem sibi
iste et iucundum reddiderit. primum temporibus
hibernis urbem Syracusas elegerat ubi ita vivebat iste
bonus imperator ut eum non modo extra tectum sed
ne extra lectum quidem quisquam viderit; ita diei brev- 5
itas conviviis, noctis longitudo stupris et flagitiis continebatur. cum autem ver esse coeperat (cuius initium
iste non a Favonio notabat, sed cum rosam viderat,
tum incipere ver arbitrabatur), dabat se labori atque
itineribus; in quibus se praebebat patientem et impi- 10
grum ut eum nemo umquam in equo sedentem viderit.
nam, ut mos fuit Bithyniae regibus, lectica octophoro
ferebatur; ipse autem coronam habebat unam in
capite, alteram in collo, reticulumque ad nares sibi
admovebat tenuissimo lino, minutis maculis, plenum 15
rosae. sic confecto itinere cum ad aliquod oppidum
venerat, eadem lectica usque in cubiculum deferebatur.
eo veniebant Siculorum magistratus, veniebant equites
Romani. controversiae secreto deferebantur, paulo
post decreta auferebantur. deinde ubi paulisper in 20
cubiculo pretio non aequitate iura discripserat, Veneri
iam et Libero reliquum tempus deberi arbitrabatur.

Cicero, *In Verrem* II.v.26-27

A Roman Governor Tours His Province

This passage is taken from Cicero's prosecution in 70 B.C. of Verres, who had been governor of Sicily from 73 B.C. to 71 B.C. and had performed his duties shamefully.

---

iudex, iudicis, m judge
accipio, ere observe, hear
iucundus, a, um pleasant
reddo, ere, reddidi make, render
temporibus hibernis in the wintertime
iste bonus imperator that fine commander: used in a derogatory or ironical manner; a Roman governor toured his province in his capacity as military commander and chief legal administrator
tectum, i, n house
5 *lectus, i, m* bed
quisquam anyone
convivium, ii, n banquet
stuprum, i, n debauchery
flagitium, ii, n scandal
continebatur Tr. "was taken up," "was consisting of"
ver, veris, n spring
sum, esse happen, take place
arbitror, ari think, believe, observe
Favonius, i, m the west wind, which blew at the commencement of spring
astrum, i, n star
noto, are mark
rosa, ae, f rose (*i.e.*, when rose petals were used at Verres' banquet table)
10 *praebeo, ere* display, show
patiens, entis hardy

impiger, impigra, impigrum energetic
mos, moris, m custom
lectica octophoro Tr. "in a litter carried by eight bearers": litters were introduced to Rome from the east and were used mainly by women and invalids and not normally at this time by able-bodied men
alteram in collo it was acceptable for a Roman to wear a garland (*coronam*) on the head but not around the neck (*collo*)
reticulum, i, n network bag, sachet
nares, ium, f nostrils
15 *tenuis, e* fine, delicate
linum, i, n linen
minutus, a, um minute, tiny
macula, ae, f mesh
aliquod some
usque in right into
defero, deferre bring away
eques, itis, m knight (*i.e.*, a businessman)
controversiae, arum, f. pl. legal disputes
20 *decreta, orum, n* decisions
paulisper for a short time
pretium, ii, n price (*i.e.*, bribes)
aequitas, atis, f fairness, impartiality
iura discripserat Tr. "had given judgements"
Liber, Liberi, m Bacchus

Hannibal Crosses the Alps

nono die in iugum Alpium perventum est per invia pleraque et errores, quos aut ducentium fraus aut temere initiae valles a coniectantibus iter faciebant. biduum in iugo fessis labore ac pugnando quies data militibus. per omnia nive oppleta cum, prima luce segniter agmen incederet et desperatio in omnium vultu emineret, Hannibal in promunturio quodam, unde longe ac late prospectus erat, consistere iussis militibus Italiam ostentat subiectosque Alpinis montibus Circumpadanos campos, moeniaque eos tum transcendere non Italiae modo sed etiam urbis Romanae; cetera plana, proclivia fore; uno aut altero proelio arcem et caput Italiae in manu ac potestate habituros.

procedere inde agmen coepit iam nihil ne hostibus quidem praeter parva furta per occasionem temptantibus. ceterum iter multo, quam in ascensu fuerat, difficilius fuit; omnis enim ferme via praeceps, angusta, lubrica erat, ut neque sustinere se ab lapsu possent aliique super alios et iumenta in homines occiderent.

ventum deinde ad multo angustiorem rupem atque ita rectis saxis ut aegre expeditus miles temptabundus manibusque retinens virgulta ac stirpes circa eminentes demittere sese posset. tandem nequiquam iumentis atque hominibus fatigatis castra in iugo posita, aegerrime ad id ipsum loco purgato: tantum nivis fodiendum atque egerendum fuit. inde ad rupem muniendam per quam unam via esse poterat milites ducti, cum caedendum esset saxum, arboribus circa immanibus deiectis struem ingentem lignorum faciunt eamque, cum et vis venti apta faciendo igni coorta est, succendunt ardentiaque saxa infuso aceto putrefaciunt. ita torridam incendio rupem ferro pandunt molliuntque anfractibus modicis clivos ut non iumenta solum sed elephanti etiam deduci possent. inferiora valles apricosque colles habent. ibi iumenta in pabulum missa et quies muniendo fessis hominibus data. triduo inde ad planum descensum.

Livy, *Ab Urbe Condita* XXI.35-37

Hannibal Crosses the Alps

In 218 B.C., the Carthaginian general Hannibal set out for Italy from Spain with 40 000 men and 37 elephants. After taking fifteen days to cross the inhospitable Alps, he reached the plains of Northern Italy with only 26 000 men.

---

iugum, i, n summit
perventum est, impers. passive they arrived
invia, orum, n. pl. trackless regions
ducentium fraus Tr. "deception of the guides"
temere, adv. by chance, blindly
coniecto, are guess
biduum, i, n two days
data (est)
5 *per omnia...habituros (esse)* a typical Latin periodic sentence with a series of subordinate ideas and actions in chronological order
nix, nivis, f snow (i.e., in late September)
oppletus, a, um covered
segniter slowly, sluggishly
agmen, inis, n army
incedo, ere advance
emineo, ere be conspicuous
promunturium, i, n ridge, ledge: there was no place in the Alps that afforded a view (*prospectus*) for Hannibal and his troops
ostento, are point out
subiectus, a, um + dat. lying below
10 *Circumpadanus, a, um* around the Po River (in North Italy)
moenia, ium, n fortifications, walls
planus, a, um flat
proclivis, e downhill
fore = futurum esse
arcem et caput citadel and capital
15 *furtum, i, n* stealthy attack
per occasionem as opportunity afforded
ferme almost
praeceps, cipitis steep
angustus, a, um narrow
lubricus, a, um slippery
sustineo, ere check, stop
lapsus, us, m slipping, falling
iumentum, i, n pack animal
occido, ere fall

20 *ventum (est), impers. passive* they came
rupes, is, f cliff
rectus, a, um steep, vertical
aegre with difficulty
expeditus, a, um unencumbered
temptabundus, a, um feeling his way
retineo, ere hold fast
virgultum, i, n bush
stirps, stirpis, f root
circa, adv. about
demitto, ere lower
castra pono, ere, posui, positus pitch camp
25 *purgatus, a, um* cleared
tantum + gen. so much
fodio, ere dig
egero, ere remove, carry away
ad rupem muniendam Tr. "to cut a path through the rock": Hannibal had to construct a path down the 300 m cliff
deiectus, a, um felled
struem lignorum pile of logs
30 *vis venti* lit., force of the wind (here, "a strong wind")
coorior, cooriri, coortus sum arise
succendo, ere kindle
ardens, entis glowing, hot
infuso aceto by pouring on vinegar: Pliny speaks of Spanish mines being worked in a similar way
putrefacio, ere, feci make crumble
torridus, a, um heated
pando, ere open up a way through
molliunt...clivos Tr. "they make the slopes less steep by short zig-zag tracks"
inferiora lower slopes
35 *apricus, a, um* sunny
pabulum, i, n pasturage
munio, ire build a road
planum, i, n plain

Oceanus

I The Tide Scatters the Fleet

iam CCCC stadia processerant, cum gubernatores agnoscere ipsos auram maris et haud procul videri sibi Oceanum abesse indicant regi. laetus rex hortari nauticos coepit ut incumberent remis. dixit adesse finem laboris omnibus votis expetitum; iam nihil gloriae deesse, nihil obstare virtuti, sine ullo Martis discrimine, sine sanguine orbem terrae ab illis capi; ne naturam quidem longius posse procedere; brevi incognita nisi immortalibus esse visuros.

tertio die mixtum flumini subibat mare, leni adhuc aestu confundente dispares undas. tum aliam insulam medio amni sitam evecti, applicant classem et ad commeatus petendos discurrunt. tertia ferme hora erat, cum stata vice Oceanus exaestuans invehi coepit et retro flumen urgere. quod primo coercitum, deinde maiore impetu adversum agebatur quam torrentia praecipiti alveo incurrunt. ignota vulgo freti natura erat, monstraque et irae deorum indicia cernere videbantur. identidem intumescens mare et in campos paulo ante siccos descendere superfusum.

iamque levatis navigiis tota classe dispersa, ei qui expositi erant, undique ad naves trepidi et improviso malo attoniti recurrunt. sed in tumultu festinatio quoque tarda est. hi contis navigia pellebant, hi, dum remos aptari prohibebant, consederant; quidam enavigare properantes, sed non exspectatis qui simul esse debebant, clauda et inhabilia navigia languide moliebantur; aliae navium inconsulte ruentes omnes receperant. ne in gubernatoribus quidem quicquam opis erat, quorum nec exaudiri vox a tumultuantibus poterat nec imperium a territis incompositisque servari.

ergo collidi inter se naves abstergerique invicem remi coeperunt. crederes non unius exercitus classem vehi, sed duorum navale inisse certamen. incutiebantur puppibus prorae, premebantur a sequentibus qui antecedentes turbaverant; iurgantium ira perveniebat etiam ad manus.

Curtius, *Historiae Alexandri* IX.ix.3-17

Oceanus

In 325 B.C., Alexander the Great sailed down the western arm of the Indus River and reached his long-sought goal of the Indian Ocean, part of Oceanus, that endless body of water that the Greeks thought surrounded the earth. Before reaching their destination, Alexander and his men encountered a tidal bore, a phenomenon similar to those that occur in rivers flowing into the Bay of Fundy.

I The Tide Scatters the Fleet

stadium, ii, n a stade: a distance of about 185 m
gubernator, oris, m helmsman, pilot
nauticus, i, m sailor
incumbo, ere lean on
5 *remus, i, m* oar
votum, i, n prayer
expetitus, a, um desired, longed for
Martis discrimine danger of war
sanguis, inis, m bloodshed
orbem terrae world
10 *subeo, ire, ii* come upon
mare, is, n sea-water
lenis, e gentle
aestus, us, m tide
confundo, ere mingle
dispares undas different waters
amnis, is, m river
applico, are land, bring ashore
classis, is, f fleet
commeatus, us, m supplies
discurro, ere run about
tertia...hora (i.e., about 9 A.M.)
ferme, adv. almost, nearly
stata vice Tr. "in its regular change"
exaestuo, are rise in flood tide, foam up
15 *retro, adv.* backwards
urgeo, ere push, force
adversum against the stream
praecipiti alveo in a downhill course
ignotus, a, um unknown: the Macedonians were probably acquainted only with the near tideless Mediterranean Sea
vulgus, i, m rank and file, common soldier
fretum, i, n sea
monstrum, i, n portent, prodigy

deum = *deorum*
cernere videbantur Tr. "they were thought to be witnessing"
intumesco, ere swell up, rise
campus, i, m plain, flat land
20 *siccus, a, um* dry
superfusum (est) overflowed
navigium, ii, n ship
levo, are, avi, atus raise
dispergo, ere, si, sus scatter
expono, ere, posui, positus set on shore
trepidus, a, um alarmed
improvisus, a, um unforeseen
malum, i, n disaster
contus, i, m pole
25 *aptari* Tr. "from being fitted in their oarlocks"
consido, ere, sedi take a seat (to row)
enavigo, are sail away
non exspectatis...debebant Tr. "without waiting for the full complement"
claudus, a, um disabled, crippled
inhabilis, e unmanageable, unwieldy
languide, adv. weakly, feebly
moliebantur were trying to get under way
inconsulte thoughtlessly, inconsiderately
30 *quicquam opis* any help
tumultuor, ari be in great confusion
incompositus, a, um disordered
abstergeo, ere shear off, break
invicem in turn
certamen, inis, n battle
incutio, ere dash against, strike into
35 *puppis, is, f* stern
prora, ae, f prow
antecedentes those preceding, in front
iurgo, are quarrel
ad manus to blows (i.e., to violence)

II Recovery and Reaching the Goal

iamque aestus totas circa flumen campos inundaverat, tumulis dumtaxat eminentibus velut insulis parvis, in quos plerique trepidi, omissis navigiis, enare properant. dispersa classis partim in praealta aqua stabat, partim in vado haerebat, cum subito novus et pristino maior terror incutitur. reciprocari coepit mare magno tractu, aquis in suum fretum recurrentibus, reddebatque terras paulo ante profundo salo mersas. igitur destituta navigia alia praecipitantur in proras, alia in latera procumbunt. strati erant campi sarcinis, armis, avulsarum tabularum remorumque fragmentis. miles nec egredi in terram nec in nave subsistere audebat identidem praesentibus graviora quae sequerentur exspectans. vix, quae perpetiebantur, videre ipsos credebant, in sicco naufragia, in amni mare.

nec finis malorum: quippe aestum paulo post mare relaturum esse, quo navigia allevarentur, ignari famem et ultima sibi ominabantur. beluae quoque fluctibus destitutae terribiles vagabantur. iamque nox appetebat, et regem quoque desperatio salutis affecerat. non tamen invictum animum curae obruunt quin tota nocte persederet in speculis equitesque praemitteret ad os amnis, ut, cum mare rursus exaestuare sensissent, praecederent. navigia quoque et lacerata refici et aversa fluctibus erigi iubet, paratosque esse et intentos, cum rursus mare terras inundavisset. tota ea nocte inter vigilias adhortationesque consumpta, celeriter et equites ingenti cursu refugere et secutus est aestus. qui primo, aquis leni tractu subeuntibus coepit levare navigia, mox, totis campis inundatis, etiam impulit classem.

plaususque militum nauticorumque insperatam salutem immodico celebrantium gaudio, litoribus ripisque resonabat. rex cum ex eo quod acciderat coniectaret post solis ortum statum tempus esse, media nocte, ut aestum occuparet, cum paucis navigiis secundo amne defluxit evectusque os eius, CCCC stadia processit in mare, tandem voti sui compos. praesidibusque et maris et locorum dis sacrificio facto, ad classem rediit.

Curtius, *Historiae Alexandri* IX.ix.18-27

II Recovery and Reaching the Goal

inundo, are flood, overflow
tumulum, i, n mound
dumtaxat only, just
emineo, ere project, stick out, protrude
omitto, ere, misi, missus abandon, desert
eno, are swim out
praealtus, a, um very deep
5 *vadum, i, n* shoal
haereo, ere be stranded, be stuck
pristinus, a, um former
incutio, ere strike
reciprocari Tr. "to ebb"
tractus, us, m pull, undertow
fretum, i, n channel
reddo, ere restore
profundus, a, um deep
salum, i, n sea-water
mersus, a, um submerged
destitutus, a, um stranded, left high and dry
praecipito, are throw upon
10 *procumbo, ere* sink down
sterno, ere, stravi, stratus strew, litter
sarcina, ae, f baggage
tabula, ae, f plank
avulsus, a, um torn away
miles, itis, m soldier: used collectively here as "soldiers"
egredior, i disembark
subsisto, ere stay aboard
perpetior, i endure, put up with
15 *siccum, i, n* dry land
naufragium, i, n shipwreck
allevo, are float
fames, is, f hunger
ultima, orum, n. pl. the end, the worst
ominor, ari foresee
belua, ae, f sea monster: possibly a crocodile
fluctus, us, m wave
vagor, ari wander

20 *appeto, ere* approach
desperatio, onis, f despair
salus, utis, f safety
invictus, a, um indomitable
obruo, ere crush
quin + subj. Tr. "so as to prevent him from"
persideo, ere, sedi continue sitting
in speculis Tr. "on the watch"
praecedo, ere outstrip, precede
laceratus, a, um damaged
reficio, ere repair
25 *aversus, a, um* overturned
erigo, ere set upright, raise
vigilia, ae, f watch
adhortatio, onis, f speech of encouragement
ingenti cursu Tr. "at full gallop"
tractus, us, m current, flow
subeo, ire come under
30 *impello, ere, impuli* set in motion
plaususque now the applause
insperatus, a, um unexpected
immodicus, a, um unrestrained
litus, oris, n shore
ripa, ae, f bank
resono, are resound
coniecto, are conjecture, guess
35 *post solis ortum* after sunrise
status, a, um regular
occupo, are catch in time, take advantage of
secundo...defluxit Tr. "he sailed downstream"
evectus, a, um having passed beyond
voti sui compos Tr. "having been granted his wishes"
praeses, idis presiding, protecting
loca, orum, n. pl. region
dis = deis

ALEXANDER'S JOURNEY IN THE DESERT

hinc pervenit ad maritimos Indos. desertam vastamque regionem late tenent ac ne cum finitimis quidem ullo commercii iure miscentur. ipsa solitudo natura quoque immitia efferavit ingenia; prominent ungues numquam recisi, comae hirsutae et intonsae sunt. tuguria conchis et ceteris purgamentis maris instruunt. ferarum pellibus tecti, piscibus sole duratis et maiorum quoque beluarum, quas fluctus eiecit, carne vescuntur. consumptis igitur alimentis Macedones primo inopiam, deinde ad ultimum famem sentire coeperunt, radices palmarum—namque sola ea arbor gignitur—ubique rimantes. sed cum haec quoque alimenta defecerant iumenta caedere aggressi ne equis quidem abstinebant. et cum deessent quae sarcinas veherent, spolia de hostibus propter quae ultima Orientis peragraverant, cremabant incendio.

famem deinde pestilentia secuta est. quippe insalubrium ciborum noxii suci, ad hoc itineris labor et aegritudo animi vulgaverant morbos, et nec manere sine clade nec progredi poterant; manentes fames, progressos acrior pestilentia urguebat. ergo strati erant campi paene pluribus semivivis quam cadaveribus. ac ne levius quidem aegri seque poterant quippe agmen raptim agebatur. igitur qui defecerant notos ignotosque ut allevarentur orabant; sed nec iumenta erant quibus excipi possent, et miles vix arma portabat, imminentisque et ipsis facies mali ante oculos erat.

rex dolore simul ac pudore anxius, quia causa tantae cladis ipse esset, ad Phrataphernen, Parthyaeorum satrapen, misit, qui iuberet camelis cocta cibaria afferri, aliosque finitimarum regionum praefectos certiores necessitatis suae fecit. nec cessatum est ab his. itaque fame dumtaxat vindicatus, exercitus tandem in Cedrosiae fines perducitur.

Curtius, Historiae Alexandri IX.x.8-18

Alexander's Journey in the Desert

In 325 B.C., Alexander crossed the 240 km Gedrosian Desert in modern Baluchistan while the fleet under Nearchus sailed along the Persian coast. After sixty days and at great cost in human life, Alexander, king and explorer, reached Mesopotamia.

maritimus, a, um coastal
teneo, ere occupy
finitimus, i, m neighbour
commercium, ii, n trade, commerce
ius, iuris, n + gen. obligations arising out of
misceo, ere (in passive) take part in, engage in
immitis, e fierce
effero, are, avi make beast-like, savage
ingenium, ii, n natural disposition, temperament
promineo, ere extend, protrude
unguis, is, m nail
5 *recisus, a, um* trimmed
coma, ae, f hair
hirsutus, a, um shaggy
intonsus, a, um unshorn, unshaved
tugurium, ii, n hut
concha, ae, f shell
ceteris purgamentis maris Tr. "other things swept in by the sea"
instruo, ere equip, furnish
pellis, is, f hide
piscis, is, m fish
duratus, a, um hardened by drying
eicio, ere cast ashore, strand
caro, carnis, f flesh
vescor, vesci + abl. feed, eat
alimentum, i, n food, provisions
10 *inopia, ae, f* scarcity
fames, is, f starvation, hunger
sentio, ire experience, suffer
radix, icis, f root
palma, ae, f palm tree
gigno, ere produce
rimor, ari rummage for
deficio, ere, feci fail

iumentum, i, n pack animal
aggredior, i, aggressus begin
abstineo, ere abstain from
sarcinae, arum, f. pl. baggage
15 *ultima* Tr. "remotest parts"
peragro, are, avi travel through
cremo, are burn
insalubris, e unwholesome
noxius, a, um harmful
sucus, i, m juice
aegritudo animi Tr. "mental depression"
vulgo, are, avi spread
morbus, i, m disease; caused by unwholesome and unprepared food
20 *clades, is, f* disaster
urgeo, ere assail
sterno, ere, stravi, stratus strew, scatter
semivivus, a, um half-alive
cadaver, eris, n dead body
levius aegri Tr. "men slightly ill"
agmen, inis, n column
25 *allevo, are* lift up
excipio, ere take
immineo, ere threaten
facies, ei, f face, spectre
malum, i, n doom, misfortune
pudor, oris, m shame
30 *satrapen, Gk. acc.* satrap: a governor of a Persian province
coctus, a, um cooked
cibaria, orum, n. pl. food
praefectus, i, m governor
certiorem facere to inform
nec cessatum est Tr. "there was no delay"
dumtaxat, adv. at least, at any rate
vindicatus, a, um delivered, freed
fines, ium, f territory

HORACE'S JOURNEY TO BRUNDISIUM

egressum magna me accepit Aricia Roma
hospitio modico: rhetor comes Heliodorus,
Graecorum longe doctissimus; inde Forum Appi,
differtum nautis, cauponibus atque malignis. . . .
hic ego propter aquam, quod erat deterrima, ventri   5
indico bellum, cenantes haud animo aequo
exspectans comites. iam nox inducere terris
umbras et caelo diffundere signa parabat.
tum pueri nautis, pueris convicia nautae
ingerere. "huc appelle!" "trecentos inseris: ohe   10
iam satis est!" dum aes exigitur, dum mula ligatur,
tota abit hora. mali culices ranaeque palustres
avertunt somnos, absentem ut cantat amicam
multa prolutus vappa nauta atque viator
certatim: tandem fessus dormire viator   15
incipit, ac missae pastum retinacula mulae
nauta piger saxo religat stertitque supinus.
iamque dies aderat, nil cum procedere lintrem
sentimus, donec cerebrosus prosilit unus
ac mulae nautaeque caput lumbosque saligno   20
fuste dolat. quarta vix demum exponimur hora.
ora manusque tua lavimus, Feronia, lympha.
milia tum pransi tria repimus atque subimus
impositum saxis late candentibus Anxur.

                              Horace, *Satires* I.v.1-26

Horace's Journey to Brundisium

In 27 B.C., the poet Horace journeyed 17 days and 580 km by way of the Via Appia from Rome south to Brundisium (Brindisi), a seaport on the Italian east coast. This passage covers the first three days, which took Horace by foot 65 km from Rome to Forum Appii and from there 28 km to Anxur (Terracina) by canal-barge pulled by mules through the Pomptine marshes.

---

magna mighty
Aricia, ae, f Aricia, a town 26 km from Rome, famous for its worship of Diana
hospitium, i, n inn
modicus, a, um modest
inde (processimus ad) from there (we went on to)
Forum Appii, n a market town 65 km from Rome, named after Appius Claudius Caecus, builder of the Via Appia (312 B.C.)
differtus, a, um crammed, swarming
nauta, ae, f boatman: Horace met the boatmen at the start of the canal-barge passage
caupo, inis, m innkeeper
malignus, a, um mean, stingy
5 *aquam* (bad water was the curse of travellers in Italy)
deterrimus, a, um worst, terrible
venter, tris, m stomach
indico, ere proclaim, declare
haud animo aequo impatiently, anxiously
diffundo, ere scatter, dot
signa, orum, n. pl. stars, constellations
puer, pueri, m slave
convicium, i, n insult
10 *ingerere, historic inf.* hurl, heap upon
huc appelle (lintrem) Tr. "put in here": the barge captain is hailed from the canal bank
trecenti, ae, a 300: a cry of outrage from a disgruntled passenger against the captain for allowing the barge to be overcrowded
insero, ere pack in, jam
ohe enough! stop!

aes, aeris, n fare
exigo, ere collect
ligo, are harness
abeo, ire vanish, go by
culex, culicis, m mosquito
ranae palustres marsh frogs
multa prolutus vappa soaked in sour wine (*i.e.*, drunk)
viator, oris, m passenger
15 *certatim* Tr. "in competition"
missae pastum Tr. "turned out to graze"
retinacula, orum, n. pl. tow ropes
piger, gra, grum lazy
religo, are tie up, fasten
sterto, ere snore
supinus, a, um on his back
linter, tris, f barge
cerebrosus, a, um hot-tempered
20 *prosilio, ire* leap (ashore)
lumbi, orum, m loins
salignus, a, um willow
fustis, is, m club
dolo, are lay into, wallop
quarta hora about 10 a.m.
demum not till
expono, ere set on shore
Feronia, ae, f an Italian goddess, consort of Jupiter at Anxur
lympha, ae, f water
pransi Tr. "after breakfast"
repo, ere crawl: Anxur (Tarracina), situated 105 km south of Rome on the west coast of Italy, was perched on a mountain with white limestone cliffs
subeo, ire draw near, approach
candens, entis gleaming, shining

Julius Caesar's First Invasion of Britain

I Invasion Preparations and the Channel Crossing

his constitutis rebus nactus idoneam ad navigandum tempestatem, tertia fere vigilia solvit, equitesque in ulteriorem portum progredi et naves conscendere et se sequi iussit. ipse hora diei circiter quarta cum primis navibus Britanniam attigit atque ibi in omnibus collibus expositas hostium copias armatas conspexit. cuius loci haec erat natura, atque ita montibus angustis mare continebatur, ut ex locis superioribus in litus telum adigi posset. hunc ad egrediendum nequaquam idoneum locum arbitratus, dum reliquae naves eo convenirent, ad horam nonam in ancoris exspectavit.

    interim legatis tribunisque militum convocatis, et quae ex Voluseno cognovisset et quae fieri vellet ostendit; monuitque ut ad nutum et ad tempus omnes res ab eis administrarentur. his dimissis, et ventum et aestum uno tempore nactus secundum, dato signo et sublatis ancoris, circiter milia passuum septem ab eo loco progressus, aperto ac plano litore naves constituit.

Caesar, De Bello Gallico IV.23

II Difficulties in Landing

at barbari, consilio Romanorum cognito, praemisso equitatu et essedariis, reliquis copiis subsecuti nostros navibus egredi prohibebant. erat ob has causas summa difficultas, quod naves propter magnitudinem nisi in alto constitui non poterant; militibus autem, ignotis locis, impeditis manibus, magno et gravi onere armorum oppressis, simul et de navibus desiliendum et in fluctibus consistendum et cum hostibus erat pugnandum; cum illi aut ex arido aut paulum in aquam progressi, omnibus membris expeditis, notissimis locis, audacter tela conicerent et equos insuefactos incitarent. quibus rebus nostri perterriti, atque huius omnino generis pugnae imperiti, non eadem alacritate ac studio, quo in pedestribus uti proeliis consueverant, utebantur.

Caesar, De Bello Gallico IV.24

Julius Caesar's First Invasion of Britain
I Invasion Preparations and the Channel Crossing

In the late summer of 55 B.C., assembling a force of eighty ships and two legions in two harbours, probably those of present-day Boulogne and Ambleteuse, 13 km to the north, Caesar set sail for Britain.

his constitutis rebus Tr. "when these matters had been arranged"
nactus, a, um having obtained
idoneus, a, um suitable
ad navigandum for sailing
tempestas, atis, f weather
fere about
tertia...vigilia (i.e., just after midnight)
vigilia, ae, f watch
solvo, ere, solvi set sail
equites, uum, m cavalry
ulterior, ius further (i.e., probably Ambleteuse)
progredior, i proceed
conscendo, ere board
hora...quarta about 9 a.m., August 26
circiter about
5 *attingo, ere, attigi* touch, reach
collis, is, m hill (i.e., probably the white cliffs of Dover)
expositus, a, um drawn up
copiae, arum, f. pl. forces
haec...ut such...that
montibus angustis by the steep cliffs
contineo, ere enclose
superior, ius higher
litus, oris, n shore
telum, i, n weapon
adigo, ere hurl
egredior, i disembark
nequaquam not at all
10 *arbitratus, a, um* judging
dum + subj. of purpose until
ad horam nonam about 3 p.m.
in ancoris at anchor
Voluseno Volusenus, Caesar's officer, had reconnoitred the British coast
ad nutum et ad tempus Tr. "at his command and on time"
15 *aestus, us, m* tide
secundus, a, um favourable
sublatis ancoris after weighing anchor
milia passuum, n. pl. miles
apertus, a, um open
planus, a, um level
constituo, ere, ui draw up

II Difficulties in Landing

praemisso...essedariis Tr. "having sent ahead the cavalry and charioteers"
subsecutus, a, um having followed closely
ob has causas on account of these reasons
nisi except
in alto in deep water
5 *militibus, dat. of agent with desiliendum (erat), ...et consistendum...et pugnandum*
impeditus, a, um encumbered, hindered
onus, eris, n weight
oppressus, a, um weighed down
desilio, ire jump down, leap down
fluctus, us, m wave
consisto, ere gain one's footing
cum illi while they (i.e., the Britons)
ex arido from dry land
10 *membrum, i, n* limb
expeditus, a, um unencumbered
conicio, ere hurl together
insuefactus, a, um trained
omnino altogether, entirely
pugna, ae, f fighting
imperitus, a, um + gen. inexperienced in
alacritas, atis, f dash, alertness
studium, i, n zeal, enthusiasm
pedester, tris, tre infantry
consuesco, ere, consuevi become accustomed

III THE LANDING

quod ubi Caesar animadvertit, naves longas, quarum species erat barbaris inusitatior, paulum removeri ab onerariis navibus et remis incitari et ad latus apertum hostium constitui atque inde fundis, sagittis, tormentis hostes propelli ac summoveri iussit; quae res magno usui nostris fuit. nam et navium figura et remorum motu et inusitato genere tormentorum permoti, barbari constiterunt ac paulum modo pedem rettulerunt.

    atque nostris militibus cunctantibus, maxime propter altitudinem maris, qui decimae legionis aquilam ferebat, contestatus deos, ut ea res legioni feliciter eveniret, "Desilite," inquit, "milites, nisi vultis aquilam hostibus prodere; ego certe meum rei publicae atque imperatori officium praestitero." hoc cum voce magna dixisset, se ex navi proiecit atque in hostes aquilam ferre coepit. tum nostri cohortati inter se, ne tantum dedecus admitteretur, universi ex navi desiluerunt.

Caesar, De Bello Gallico IV.25

IV CAESAR WINS CONTROL

pugnatum est ab utrisque acriter. nostri tamen, quod neque ordines servare neque firmiter insistere neque signa subsequi poterant, magnopere perturbabantur; hostes vero, notis omnibus vadis, incitatis equis nostros impeditos adoriebantur, plures paucos circumsistebant, alii ab latere aperto in universos tela coniciebant.

    quod cum animadvertisset Caesar, scaphas longarum navium, item speculatoria navigia militibus compleri iussit et, quos laborantes conspexerat, his subsidia summittebat. nostri, simul in arido constiterunt, suis omnibus consecutis, in hostes impetum fecerunt atque eos in fugam dederunt; neque longius prosequi potuerunt, quod equites cursum tenere atque insulam capere non potuerant. hoc unum ad pristinam fortunam Caesari defuit.

Caesar, De Bello Gallico IV.26

III The Landing

quod = co-ordinating *relative* this
navis longa, f warship
inusitatior quite unfamiliar
removeri...summoveri five present passive infinitives dependent on *iussit*
navis oneraria, f transport
remis incitari Tr. "to be rowed hard"
latus, eris, n flank, side
apertus, a, um exposed (i.e., the right flank, the side unprotected by the shield)
inde from that position
funda, ae, f sling: this weapon could fire stones up to about 35 m
sagitta, ae, f arrow
5 *tormentum, i, n* artillery (i.e., on the ship's decks)
propello, ere drive off, repel
summoveo, ere dislodge
quae res this manoeuvre
figura, ae, f shape
inusitatus, a, um strange, unfamiliar
permotus, a, um alarmed, disturbed
consisto, ere, stiti halt
paulum modo only a little way

pedem refero, referre, rettuli retreat
cunctor, ari hesitate, delay
10 *altitudo, inis, f* depth
qui = *is qui* he who
aquila, ae, f eagle: the eagle was the standard of the legion; the *signa* were the standards of each military unit (*cohort*, *maniple*, and *century*); in battle, the standards with musical instruments were used to relay messages such as advance, retreat, or rally
contestor, ari, atus sum call to witness
feliciter fortunately
evenio, ire turn out
prodo, ere betray
res publica, rei publicae, f state
imperator, oris, m general
officium, i, n duty
praesto, are, stiti discharge
15 *proicio, ere, ieci* fling oneself forth
cohortati inter se encouraging one another
dedecus, oris, n disgrace
admitto, ere incur, commit
universus, a, um all together, in a body

IV Caesar Wins Control

pugnatum est, impersonal passive Tr. "the battle was fought"
uterque, utraque, utrumque both sides
nostri...coniciebant (lines 1-6) a typical periodic sentence
ordines servare preserve or keep the ranks
firmiter insistere get a firm footing
subsequor, i follow closely
perturbo, are throw into confusion
vadum, i, n shallow
5 *adorior, adoriri* attack
circumsisto, ere surround, crowd around
scapha, ae, f skiff (i.e., the ship's boats)

item likewise
speculatoria navigia, n. pl. scouting ships
laboro, are be in distress
subsidia, orum, n reinforcements
10 *summittebat* Tr. "kept sending"
consisto, ere, stiti keep one's position
consequor, i, secutus sum pursue
neque longius no further
prosequor, i follow after
cursus, us, m course
insulam capere Tr. "to reach the island"
pristinus, a, um usual
15 *desum, deesse, defui* lack

Daedalus and Icarus

I Preparations for the Flight

Daedalus interea Creten longumque perosus
exsilium, tactusque loci natalis amore,
clausus erat pelago. "terras licet" inquit "et undas
obstruat, at caelum certe patet; ibimus illac!
omnia possideat, non possidet aera Minos."   5
dixit et ignotas animum dimittit in artes,
naturamque novat. nam ponit in ordine pennas,
ut clivo crevisse putes; sic rustica quondam
fistula disparibus paulatim surgit avenis.
tum lino medias et ceris adligat imas,   10
atque ita compositas parvo curvamine flectit,
ut veras imitetur aves. puer Icarus una
stabat et, ignarus sua se tractare pericla,
ore renidenti modo, quas vaga moverat aura,
captabat plumas, flavam modo pollice ceram   15
mollibat, lusuque suo mirabile patris
impediebat opus. postquam manus ultima coepto
imposita est, geminas opifex libravit in alas
ipse suum corpus motaque pependit in aura.
instruit et natum "medio" que "ut limite curras, 20
Icare," ait "moneo, ne, si demissior ibis,
unda gravet pennas, si celsior, ignis adurat.
inter utrumque vola! nec te spectare Booten
aut Helicen iubeo strictumque Orionis ensem:
me duce carpe viam!" pariter praecepta volandi   25
tradit et ignotas umeris accommodat alas.

Ovid, Metamorphoses VIII.183-209

Daedalus and Icarus

Daedalus, an Athenian master craftsman, built a labyrinth for Minos, King of Crete, who subsequently kept him prisoner on the island. After many years' imprisonment, Daedalus resolved to try to escape from the island by air with his son, Icarus.

I Preparations for the Flight

perosus, a, um hating intensely
locus natalis, loci natalis, m native land (i.e., Athens)
claudo, ere, clausi, clausus cut off
pelagus, i, n sea
licet although
at nevertheless
pateo, ere lie open
illac by that way
5 *aer, aeris, m* air
ignotus, a, um unknown
animum dimittit Tr. "directs his attention"
novo, are revolutionize, alter
penna, ae, f feather
clivus, i, m slope
crevisse = pennas crevisse
cresco, ere, crevi grow
quondam sometimes
fistula, ae, f pipe
dispar, disparis of different length
paulatim gradually
surgo, ere be built up, grow up
avena, ae, f reed
10 *linum, i, n* thread
medias (pennas) et...imas (pennas)
cera, ae, f wax
adligo, are bind together, fasten
imus, a, um bottom
compositus, a, um arranged
curvamen, inis, n curve
flecto, ere bend
imitor, ari imitate
una with him, beside him
sua...pericla cause of peril for himself
tracto, are handle
renidens, entis cheerful, beaming for joy
vagus, a, um wandering
aura, ae, f breeze
15 *captabat* Tr. "he repeatedly tried to catch"

pluma, ae, f feather
flavus, a, um golden yellow
pollex, icis, m thumb
mollibat = molliebat was softening
lusus, us, m games, play
manus ultima Tr. "the finishing touch"
coeptum, i, n undertaking
impono, ere, imposui, impositus put on
geminus, a, um two
opifex, icis, m craftsman (i.e., Daedalus)
libro, are, avi balance
ala, ae, f wing
pendo, ere, pependi hover, hang suspended
20 *instruo, ere* equip, fit (with wings)
natus, i, m son
medio...limite Tr. "by the middle course"
curro, ere fly, hasten
demissior too low
gravo, are weigh down
celsior too high
ignis, is, m heat of the sun (lit., fire)
aduro, ere burn
utrumque Tr. "the two extremes"
volo, are fly
Booten the constellations Bootes, the Bear Keeper, Orion, the Great Hunter, and Helice, the Great Bear (the Big Dipper) are the most conspicuous groups of stars in the northern heavens and were particularly useful to sailors as navigational signs
strictus, a, um unsheathed
ensis, is, m sword
25 *carpo, ere* take one's way
pariter at the same time
praeceptum, i, n instruction
umerus, i, m shoulder
accommodo, are fasten

II THE FLIGHT

inter opus monitusque genae maduere seniles,
et patriae tremuere manus. dedit oscula nato
non iterum repetenda suo, pennisque levatus
ante volat comitique timet, velut ales, ab alto
quae teneram prolem produxit in aera nido; 5
hortaturque sequi, damnosasque erudit artes,
et movet ipse suas et nati respicit alas.
hos aliquis tremula dum captat harundine pisces,
aut pastor baculo stivave innixus arator
vidit et obstipuit, quique aethera carpere possent, 10
credidit esse deos. et iam Iunonia laeva
parte Samos (fuerant Delosque Parosque relictae),
dextra Lebinthos erat fecundaque melle Calymne,
cum puer audaci coepit gaudere volatu
deseruitque ducem, caelique cupidine tractus 15
altius egit iter. rapidi vicinia solis
mollit odoratas, pennarum vincula, ceras.
tabuerant cerae; nudos quatit ille lacertos,
remigioque carens non ullas percipit auras.
oraque caerulea patrium clamantia nomen 20
excipiuntur aqua, quae nomen traxit ab illo.
at pater infelix nec iam pater, "Icare," dixit,
"Icare," dixit "ubi es? qua te regione requiram?"
"Icare," dicebat; pennas aspexit in undis,
devovitque suas artes corpusque sepulcro 25
condidit, et tellus a nomine dicta sepulti.

                Ovid, *Metamorphoses* VIII.210-235

II The Flight

inter during
monitus, us, m warning
gena, ae, f cheek
madesco, ere, madui become wet
senilis, e old
patrius, a, um of the father
non iterum repetenda never again to be repeated
levatus, a, um raised
ante in front, before
velut like
ales, is, f bird
5 *tener, tenera, tenerum* helpless, tender
proles, prolis, f offspring, fledgling
produco, ere, duxi lead forth
nidus, i, m nest
damnosus, a, um fatal
erudio, ire teach
tremulus, a, um quivering
harundo, inis, f rod
piscis, is, m fish
baculum, i, n staff, crook
stiva, ae, f plough-handle
-ve or
innixus, a, um leaning on
arator, oris, m ploughman
10 *obstipesco, ere, obstipui* be astounded
aethera, Gk. acc. air
carpo, ere fly through
Iunonia sacred to Juno: Juno had a famous temple on Samos, an island off the coast of Turkey
laeva parte on the left side
Delos, Paros, Lebinthus, Calymne islands in the Aegean

fecunda...melle Tr. "abundant in honey"
gaudeo, ere rejoice, take pleasure in
volatus, us, m the act of flying, flight
15 *tractus, a, um* drawn on, urged on
altius egit iter Tr. "he steered too high a course"
rapidus, a, um blazing, scorching
vicinia, ae, f nearness
mollio, ire soften
odoratus, a, um scented, fragrant
vinculum, i, n fastening
tabesco, ere, tabui melt
quatio, ere flap, shake
lacertus, i, m arm
remigio...carens Tr. "lacking wings" (lit., "lacking oars")
ullus, a, um any
percipio, ere catch hold of
20 *os, oris, n* mouth
caeruleus, a, um blue or greenish blue
excipio, ere receive
traxit Tr. "derived"
nec iam no longer
requiro, ere search for
dicebat Tr. "kept saying"
aspicio, ere, aspexi look at, behold, see
25 *devoveo, ere, devovi* curse
condo, ere, condidi bury, inter
tellus, uris, f land: Icaria, an island west of Samos
dicta (est) was called
sepultus, a, um the one who was buried

43

PART III: TRAVEL BY LAND, WATER, AND AIR

Initial Questions

A Roman Governor Tours His Province
1. How did Verres' view of the arrival of spring differ from the ordinary Roman's? Account for this difference.
2. Why does Cicero repeat the word *"labor"* in this passage?
3. How does Verres settle disputes?
4. Cicero's chief method of attacking Verres is ridicule. Provide two examples of this technique and explain them.
5. What emerges from this passage about the character of Verres?

Hannibal Crosses the Alps
1. Suppose you were a soldier in Hannibal's army. Describe the difficulties that you and others (including animals) encountered on the journey up to and down from the Alpine summit. Why was the descent more difficult than the ascent?
2. What discouraging signs did the soldiers exhibit as they set out at dawn from the summit? What words of encouragement did Hannibal use at a vantage point to improve his troops' morale?
3. What rhetorical devices does Livy use to make Hannibal's speech effective?
4. How did Hannibal overcome the natural obstacle of a precipice? Outline the stages of the skilful operation.
5. How long did Hannibal's journey take? Why has Hannibal's trek captured the imagination of later generations?

I The Tide Scatters the Fleet
1. How does Curtius use the rhetorical devices of balance and repetition to make Alexander's speech so effective? What immediate effect did the speech have on his men?
2. What words and images best describe the impact of the tidal wave on the men and ships?
3. What does Curtius mean by the sentence *"sed in tumultu festinatio quoque tarda est"*?
4. Why were the rescue efforts by the ships so ineffective?

II Recovery and Reaching the Goal
1. What remained after the sea flowed back and restored the Indus waters to their normal channel?
2. What precautions did Alexander successfully take to prevent further disaster to his men and ships?
3. How did the sailors account for the sudden change in the tide? How did Alexander?
4. Does Curtius provide the reader with a cameraman's description of events? Divide the passage into camera "shots" and explain how the picture is built up.
5. Is Curtius always "objective" in his description or is he "subjective"?

Alexander's Journey in the Desert
1. How does Curtius' use of diction, emphatic word order, repetition, and imagery dramatically describe the desolation of the region, the uncivilized nature of the Indi tribe, and the different stages of desperation that the Macedonians felt as they crossed the Gedrosian desert?
2. Why did Alexander express grief and shame during the journey?

Horace's Journey to Brundisium
1. How does Horace make use of contrast in lines 1 to 4?
2. What two activities on the barge took a whole hour?
3. When the passengers woke up what did they find?
4. How long did the journey take by barge?
5. What physical discomforts did Horace face on his land and water journey? Are his discomforts entirely foreign to us today?
6. Pick out the words and phrases Horace uses in providing a travelogue. How successful has he been in avoiding a monotonous account of his travel experiences?
7. What satirical elements are found in this genuinely amusing episode?

I Invasion Preparations and the Channel Crossing
1. Describe the position chosen by the Britons at the time of Caesar's landing.
2. What instructions did Caesar give to his legates and tribunes?

II Difficulties in Landing
1. What three difficulties did Caesar's men encounter during the landing on the coast of Kent?
2. What advantages did the enemy have in repelling Caesar's landing?
3. What words does Caesar use to describe the impact of the Britons' attack on his men?

III The Landing
1. How did the invasion forces achieve a successful landing? Consider the role of the standard-bearer of the Tenth Legion and the tactics of Caesar.

IV Caesar Wins Control
1. How were the Romans able to put the enemy to flight?
2. After the landing, why wasn't Caesar able to pursue the enemy?
3. What qualities of generalship does Caesar display in this passage?
4. Examine Caesar's writing style under the following topics: (1) the reason for using direct speech in the middle of his narrative; (2) the use of long periodic sentences in his narration.
5. Which parts of Caesar's commentary are more clearly visualized by the reader? Why?
6. What feelings does the passage arouse in you towards (a) Caesar? (b) the standard-bearer? (c) the legionary? (d) the enemy?

I Preparations for the Flight
1. Why was it difficult for Daedalus and Icarus to escape from Crete?
2. What materials and steps were involved in shaping the wings?
3. While his father constructs the wings, how does Icarus entertain himself?
4. How does Ovid emphasize the joy, marvel, and potential danger in Daedalus' new creation?
5. What last-minute briefing does Daedalus give to his son? Why are the different constellations mentioned in the father's instructions to his son? Why is the briefing so detailed?
6. Why does Ovid describe Daedalus as *ducem* rather than *patrem*?
7. Comment on the poet's use of the following words and phrases: *longum exsilium* (lines 1-2), *ignotas artes* (line 6), *naturam novat* (line 7), *ignarus* (line 13), *medio limite* (line 20).

II The Flight
1. What emotions does Daedalus exhibit while talking to Icarus?
2. Before he begins to fly what action does Daedalus perform? How appropriate is the simile that describes Daedalus' action in lines 4 and 5?
3. Describe: a) the path of the aeronauts' flight (consult the map on page 16), b) the onlookers and their reaction to the flight, and c) Icarus' fall from the sky.
4. What was Icarus' mistake? Why did he make it? How does Ovid describe the impact of the mistake on the wings of Icarus, Icarus himself, and his father?
5. Comment on the poet's use of the following words and phrases: *damnosas artes* (line 6), *credidit esse deos* (line 11), *caeli cupidine* (line 15), *nudos lacertos* (line 18), and *remigio* (line 19).
6. Examine Ovid's use of diction, split phrases, repetition, irony, simile, parallelism, and images. How does each poetic device contribute to the impact of the theme?
7. Which character do you find more attractive and lifelike —Daedalus or Icarus? Explain your answer. Are the two an example of a generation gap?

Discussion Questions
1. Compare Ovid's account of the fall of Icarus with the paintings by the artists Brueghel, Allegrini, Saraceni, Rubens and Michael Ayrton. How is each painter's version similar to or different from Ovid's account?
2. What motives did Caesar, Hannibal, and Alexander have for travelling?
3. What travel conditions did Caesar, Cicero, Alexander, Hannibal, Horace, Daedalus and Icarus encounter in their journeys? What effects did these conditions have on the people involved?
4. What indications does the reader have that the generals displayed excellent leadership? What leadership skills did they possess in common? Do you admire them?

5. The literary craft of Curtius, Livy, and Ovid is characterized by an easily followed exposition, striking features, dramatic effects, and a preoccupation with psychological considerations. Discuss this statement in the light of the selections you have read. Are there scenes or images that you find (a) clearer, (b) more dramatic and exciting, (c) objective, (d) subjective? If so, why?
6. Imagine you are a soldier in Hannibal's or Caesar's or Alexander's army. Write a letter home to a friend or wife, telling about your adventures.
7. Compare Cicero, Livy, and Horace as writers: consider each author's treatment of a similar theme and his attitude and intention in writing about travel.
9. To develop a better understanding of the problems of travelling in the ancient world, examine a map and, using the map scale, determine:
   (a) the route of Paulus' journey;
   (b) the land distance between various places on Alexander's journey: e.g., Pella to Alexandria; Alexandria to Ecbatana to Samarkand; Pattala to Pura to Persepolis to Susa to Babylon; Babylon to Alexandria;
   (c) the water distance between Taxila and Babylon;
   (d) the types of terrain encountered by Alexander in his travels;
   (e) Hannibal's route through the Alps.
10. For centuries readers and artists have enjoyed Daedalus and Icarus' flight of fantasy. Why? Is it because the myth symbolizes some basic aspect of human nature? Has space exploration today with its own heroes and tragedies rekindled an interest in this myth? Or is there some other reason?

Further Readings

Catullus describes the final voyage of his yacht (*Carmina 4*), and a poem ascribed to Vergil provides a parody of that voyage with its adventure of a muleteer (*Catalepton* X).

Selected passages from Nepos' *Hannibal*.

PART IV
A JOURNEY THROUGH THE UNDERWORLD

(SELECTED PASSAGES FROM VERGIL'S *AENEID*, BOOK SIX)

Vergil's Underworld

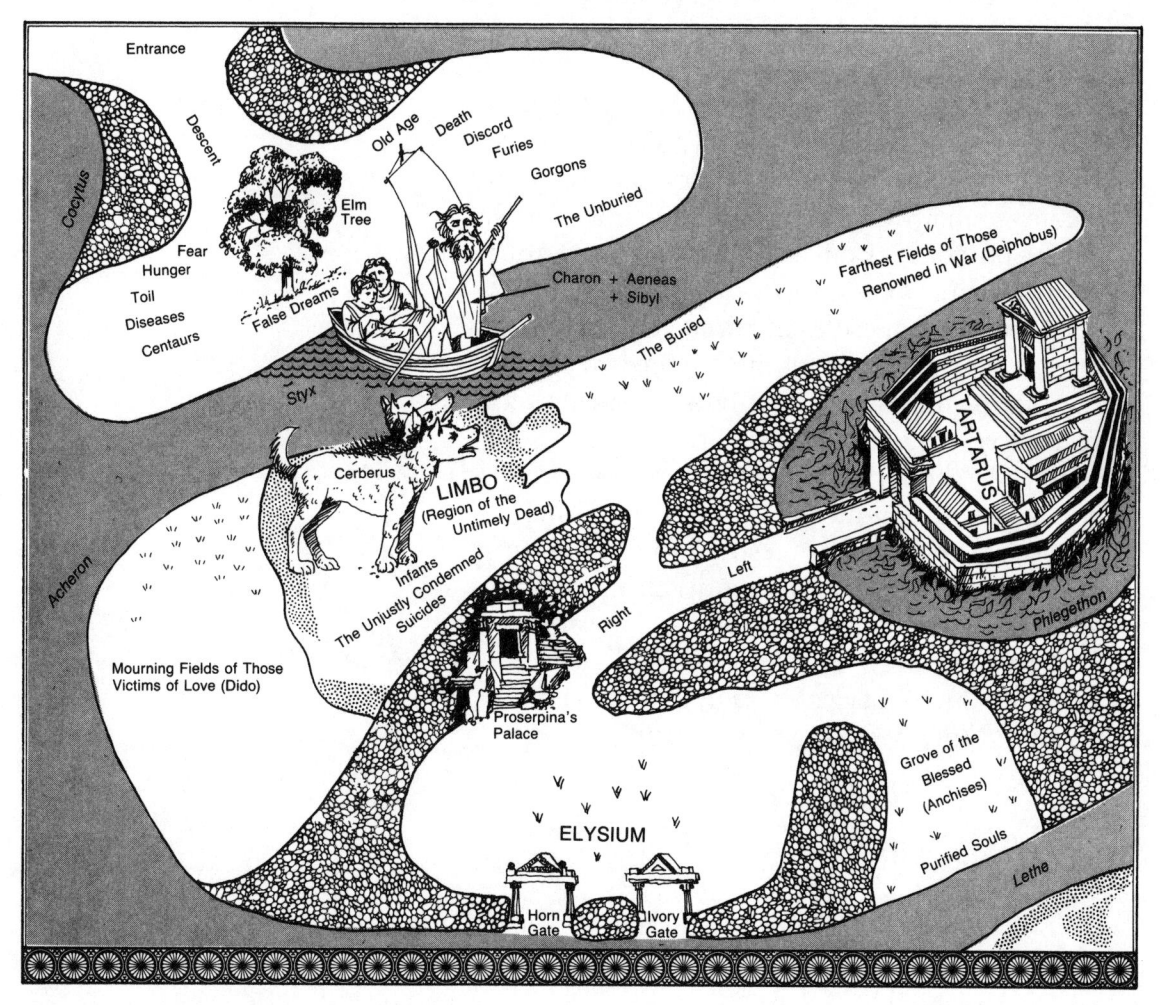

THE DESCENT TO THE UNDERWORLD

talibus orabat dictis arasque tenebat,
cum sic orsa loqui vates: "sate sanguine divum,
Tros Anchisiade, facilis descensus Averno:
noctes atque dies patet atri ianua Ditis;
sed revocare gradum superasque evadere ad auras, 5
hoc opus, hic labor est. pauci, quos aequus amavit
Iuppiter aut ardens evexit ad aethera virtus,
dis geniti potuere. tenent media omnia silvae,
Cocytusque sinu labens circumvenit atro.
quod si tantus amor menti, si tanta cupido est 10
bis Stygios innare lacus, bis nigra videre
Tartara, et insano iuvat indulgere labori,
accipe quae peragenda prius. latet arbore opaca
aureus et foliis et lento vimine ramus,
Iunoni infernae dictus sacer; hunc tegit omnis 15
lucus et obscuris claudunt convallibus umbrae.
sed non ante datur telluris operta subire
auricomos quam quis decerpserit arbore fetus.
hoc sibi pulchra suum ferri Proserpina munus
instituit. primo avulso non deficit alter 20
aureus, et simili frondescit virga metallo.
ergo alte vestiga oculis et rite repertum
carpe manu; namque ipse volens facilisque sequetur,
si te fata vocant; aliter non viribus ullis
vincere nec duro poteris convellere ferro. 25
praeterea iacet exanimum tibi corpus amici
(heu nescis) totamque incestat funere classem,
dum consulta petis nostroque in limine pendes.
sedibus hunc refer ante suis et conde sepulcro.
duc nigras pecudes; ea prima piacula sunto. 30
sic demum lucos Stygis et regna invia vivis
aspicies." dixit, pressoque obmutuit ore.

                                          Lines 124-155

The Descent to the Underworld

After landing at Cumae, 16 km west of Naples, Aeneas visits in her cave the Sibyl, the priestess of Apollo. Aeneas requests to visit his father Anchises in the underworld. In this passage, the Sibyl outlines the two conditions before the Trojan leader can enter Hades.

---

orsa (est) began
satus, a, um born of, sprung from
divum = divorum; divus, i, m god: an archaic form to give a touch of realism
Anchisiade Tr. "son of Anchises"
descensus, us, m descent
Avernus, i, m (Lake) Avernus, near Cumae, inspired the ancient belief that it led to the underworld because of its depth and foul smell and the surrounding gloomy-looking woods
Dis, itis, m Pluto, lord of the underworld
5 *revoco, are* retrace
superas...ad auras Tr. "to the air above"
evado, ere escape
aequus, a, um kind, favouring
eveho, ere, evexi exalt, lift up
aethera, Gk. acc. sing. upper air, heaven
virtus, utis, f worth, excellence
dis geniti Tr. "sons of gods"
media omnia Tr. "the whole intervening space" (i.e., between the upper and lower world)
Cocytus, i, m the four rivers of hell were Cocytus (lamentation), Styx (hate), Phlegethon (burning), and Acheron (pain)
sinus, us, m winding course
labor, labi glide
11 *inno, are* sail upon
accipio, ere hear, learn
peragenda (sint) must be accomplished
opacus, a, um shady
folium, i, n leaf
lentus, a, um pliant
vimen, inis, n twig
ramus, i, m bough
15 *Iunoni infernae* Tr. "to Juno of the lower world" (i.e., Proserpina)
lucus, i, m grove

convallis, is, f valley
telluris operta Tr. "earth's hidden places"
auricomus, a, um golden-haired
quis = aliquis someone
decerpo, ere, decerpsi remove by plucking, pick
fetus, us, m growth
20 *instituo, ere, ui* ordain
avello, ere, velli, vulsus pluck off, tear away
deficio, ere lack
frondesco, ere bear leaves
virga, ae, f branch
ergo...manu Tr. "So search with your eyes on high, and when you have found (the bough) duly pull it away with your hand"
rite duly: this word marks the religious aspect of Aeneas's quest
aliter otherwise
25 *convello, ere* tear away
exanimus, a, um lifeless
incesto, are pollute
funus, eris, n death
classis, is, f fleet
consulta, orum, n. pl. decisions, advice
sedibus...suis in his resting place
refer duly place
ante first
condo, ere bury
30 *nigras* black (*niger*) victims were always offered to gods of the dead
pecudes, um, f cattle
ea...sunto let these be
piacula, orum, n. pl. purifying sacrifices
demum at last
invius, a, um pathless
aspicio, ere behold
pressoque...ore with her lips fast closed
obmutesco, ere, obmutui fall silent

The Portals of Hades

ibant obscuri sola sub nocte per umbram
perque domos Ditis vacuas et inania regna:
quale per incertam lunam sub luce maligna
est iter in silvis, ubi caelum condidit umbra
Iuppiter, et rebus nox abstulit atra colorem.　　　　5
vestibulum ante ipsum primisque in faucibus Orci
Luctus et ultrices posuere cubilia Curae,
pallentesque habitant Morbi tristisque Senectus,
et Metus et malesuada Fames ac turpis Egestas,
terribiles visu formae, Letumque Labosque;　　　　10
tum consanguineus Leti Sopor et mala mentis
Gaudia, mortiferumque adverso in limine Bellum,
ferreique Eumenidum thalami et Discordia demens
vipereum crinem vittis innexa cruentis.
in medio ramos annosaque bracchia pandit　　　　15
ulmus opaca, ingens, quam sedem Somnia vulgo
vana tenere ferunt, foliisque sub omnibus haerent.
multaque praeterea variarum monstra ferarum,
Centauri in foribus stabulant Scyllaeque biformes
et centumgeminus Briareus ac belua Lernae　　　　20
horrendum stridens, flammisque armata Chimaera,
Gorgones Harpyiaeque et forma tricorporis umbrae.
corripit hic subita trepidus formidine ferrum
Aeneas strictamque aciem venientibus offert,
et ni docta comes tenues sine corpore vitas　　　　25
admoneat volitare cava sub imagine formae,
inruat et frustra ferro diverberet umbras.

　　　　　　　　　　　　　Lines 268-294

The Portals of Hades

Assisted by his mother Venus, Aeneas complies with the Sibyl's conditions and enters a deep cave which, leading down to the underworld, is protected by Lake Avernus and a gloomy forest. Travelling through darkness, Aeneas and the Sibyl are confronted by monsters and countless forms of human suffering at the cave entrance.

---

obscurus, a, um dim, shrouded in darkness
solus, a, um lonely
umbra, ae, f shadow
vacuus, a, um empty, void
inanis, e unsubstantial, phantom, ghostly
quale iter like a journey
malignus, a, um scanty, poor
condo, ere, condidi hide, blanket
5 *fauces, ium, f* entrance, jaws
Orcus, i, m underworld: normally the word means Orcus (Pluto), god of the underworld
Luctus, us, m Grief, Anguish
ultrix, icis avenging
cubile, is, n bed
pallens, entis pale
Senectus, utis, f Old Age
Metus, us, m Fear
malesuadus, a, um evil-counselling
turpis, e disgraceful, unsightly
Egestas, atis, f Poverty, Need
10 *terribiles visu formae* shapes frightful to see
Letum, i, n Death
Labos, archaic form of Labor Toil, Hardship
consanguineus, i, m brother
Sopor, oris, m Sleep
Eumenides, um, f. pl. the Furies: the avenging Furies were fearful winged women with snakes entangled in their bodies and hair who punished evildoers for violations such as disobeying one's parents, perjury, or murder
thalamus, i, m chamber
demens, entis mad
vipereus, a, um snaky
crinis, is, m hair
vitta, ae, f headband
innexus, a, um entwined
cruentus, a, um bloody

15 *annosus, a, um* aged
bracchium, ii, n branch
pando, ere stretch out, spread
ulmus, i, f elm-tree: the dwelling place of empty dreams
opacus, a, um shady
vulgo...ferunt they commonly say
vanus, a, um empty, idle, insubstantial
fera, ae, f wild beast
Centaurus, i, m the Centaur: a creature that was half man and half horse
stabulo, are be stabled
Scylla, ae, f Scylla: a sea monster, half-woman, half-serpent, with a dog's bark
biformis, e two-formed, two-shaped
20 *centumgeminus Briareus* hundredfold Briareus
belua Lernae the beast of Lerna was the hydra or water snake slain by Hercules
stridens, entis hissing
Chimaera a tripartite dragon, one-third lion, one-third goat, and one-third snake
Gorgo, onis, f Gorgon: Medusa and her sisters were monsters with snaky hair and terrible faces whose gazes killed or turned to stone
Harpyiae, arum, f. pl. Harpies were birds with faces of women
tricorporis umbrae of the three-bodied phantom (i.e., Geryon, a monster slain by Hercules)
corripio, ere snatch, seize, grasp
formido, inis, f fear
strictus, a, um bare, unsheathed
acies, ei, f edge
25 *ni = nisi*
tenuis, e unsubstantial
vita, ae, f spirit, shade
volito, are fly about, flutter
cavus, a, um hollow
diverbero, are strike violently, cut, hack

CHARON, FERRYMAN OF THE DEAD

portitor has horrendus aquas et flumina servat
terribili squalore Charon, cui plurima mento
canities inculta iacet, stant lumina flamma,
sordidus ex umeris nodo dependet amictus.
ipse ratem conto subigit velisque ministrat 5
et ferruginea subvectat corpora cumba,
iam senior, sed cruda deo viridisque senectus.
huc omnis turba ad ripas effusa ruebat,
matres atque viri defunctaque corpora vita
magnanimum heroum, pueri innuptaeque puellae, 10
impositique rogis iuvenes ante ora parentum:
quam multa in silvis autumni frigore primo
lapsa cadunt folia, aut ad terram gurgite ab alto
quam multae glomerantur aves, ubi frigidus annus
trans pontum fugat et terris immittit apricis. 15
stabant orantes primi transmittere cursum
tendebantque manus ripae ulterioris amore.
navita sed tristis nunc hos nunc accipit illos,
ast alios longe summotos arcet harena.
                              Lines 298-316

CERBERUS

Cerberus haec ingens latratu regna trifauci
personat adverso recubans immanis in antro.
cui vates horrere videns iam colla colubris
melle soporatam et medicatis frugibus offam
obicit. ille fame rabida tria guttura pandens 5
corripit obiectam, atque immania terga resolvit
fusus humi totoque ingens extenditur antro.
occupat Aeneas aditum custode sepulto
evaditque celer ripam inremeabilis undae.
                              Lines 417-425

Charon, Ferryman of the Dead

The grim ferryman, Charon, waits at the River Styx to take across those who have been buried.

portitor, oris, m ferryman
horrendus, a, um grim, dreadful
cui mento Tr. "on whose chin"
canities, is, f grey hair
incultus, a, um unkempt, untrimmed
sto, are be fixed
lumina, um, n. pl. eyes
nodus, i, m knot
dependeo, ere hang down
amictus, us, m cloak
5 *ratis, is, f* boat, craft
contus, i, m pole
subigo, ere push along, punt
velum, i, n sail
ministro, are attend to, trim
ferrugineus, a, um rust-coloured
subvecto, are carry, transport
cumba, ae, f boat, bark
crudus, a, um fresh, vigorous
viridis, e green
ripa, ae, f bank
defunctus, a, um + abl. finished, ended
10 *magnanimum, gen. pl.* noble in spirit, brave

innuptus, a, um unwed
rogus, i, m funeral pyre
quam multa as many as
lapsus, a, um gliding down
folium, i, n leaf
gurges, itis, m flood, torrent
glomero, are mass together, flock
frigidus annus cold season
15 *pontus, i, m* sea
apricus, a, um sunny
tendo, ere stretch out: Virgil's image in lines 16-19 can be compared to people in any large city who hurry en masse in rush hour to the subway platform to wait anxiously and then crowd around the train entrance in the hope of boarding it
ulterior, ius farther
amor, oris, m longing, yearning
ast = at but, however
summotus, a, um moved away, waved back
arceo, ere + abl. keep away
harena, ae, f sand

Cerberus

After Aeneas and the Sibyl show their passport to the underworld, the Golden Bough, Charon reluctantly ferries his "live" passengers over to the other bank where Cerberus, the three-headed watchdog of Pluto's domain, waits.

latratus, us, m barking
trifaucis, -is, -e triple-throated
persono, are make resound
adversus, a, um facing
recubo, are lie, sprawl
horreo, ere bristle
collum, i, n neck
coluber, bri, m snake, serpent
mel, mellis, n honey
soporatus, a, um made drowsy
medicatus, a, um drugged
fruges, um, f. pl. meal, grain

offa, ae, f titbit, morsel
5 *obicio, ere, obieci, obiectus* throw before
guttur, is, n throat
pando, ere open
corripio, ere catch
resolvo, ere, resolvi relax
fusus Tr. "as he sank down"
sepulto (somno) buried (in sleep)
evado, ere pass beyond
inremeabilis from which there is no return
unda, ae, f stream

TARTARUS

respicit Aeneas subito et sub rupe sinistra
moenia lata videt triplici circumdata muro,
quae rapidus flammis ambit torrentibus amnis,
Tartareus Phlegethon, torquetque sonantia saxa.
porta adversa ingens solidoque adamante columnae, 5
vis ut nulla virum, non ipsi exscindere bello
caelicolae valeant; stat ferrea turris ad auras,
Tisiphoneque sedens palla succincta cruenta
vestibulum exsomnis servat noctesque diesque.
hinc exaudiri gemitus et saeva sonare 10
verbera, tum stridor ferri tractaeque catenae.
constitit Aeneas strepitumque exterritus hausit.
"quae scelerum facies? o virgo, effare; quibusve
urgentur poenis? quis tantus plangor ad auras?"
tum vates sic orsa loqui:... 15
"hic, quibus invisi fratres, dum vita manebat,
pulsatusve parens et fraus innexa clienti,
aut qui divitiis soli incubuere repertis
nec partem posuere suis (quae maxima turba est),
quique ob adulterium caesi, quique arma secuti 20
impia nec veriti dominorum fallere dextras,
inclusi poenam exspectant. ne quaere doceri
quam poenam, aut quae forma viros fortunave mersit.
saxum ingens volvunt alii, radiisque rotarum
districti pendent; sedet aeternumque sedebit 25
infelix Theseus, Phlegyasque miserrimus omnes
admonet et magna testatur voce per umbras:
'discite iustitiam moniti et non temnere divos.'
vendidit hic auro patriam dominumque potentem
imposuit; fixit leges pretio atque refixit; 30
hic thalamum invasit natae vetitosque hymenaeos:
ausi omnes immane nefas ausoque potiti.
non, mihi si linguae centum sint oraque centum,
ferrea vox, omnis scelerum comprendere formas,
omnia poenarum percurrere nomina possim." 35

                        Lines 548-562; 608-627

Tartarus

Quickly passing by Cerberus, the Sibyl and Aeneas travel through Limbo, the region of those who died before their time. Next, at a juncture or point where the road divides, Aeneas sees to the left the fortress of Tartarus, the abode of the damned, and is told by the Sibyl about the sinners and their punishments.

---

rupes, is, f rock
moenia, ium, n Tr. "buildings"
circumdatus, a, um surrounded
ambio, ire encircle
torrens, entis hot, scorching, roaring
amnis, is, m river
Phlegethon the burning river of the underworld
torqueo, ere whirl along, roll
sonans, antis echoing
5 *adversus, a, um* in front
adamas, antis, m (mythological) the hardest of all substances, adamant, perhaps hard steel
virum = *virorum*
exscindo, ere destroy
caelicola, ae, m heavendweller
valeo, ere have the strength
turris, is, f tower
Tisiphone one of the Furies, the avenger of murder
palla, ae, f mantle, robe
succinctus, a, um wrapped, clothed
cruentus, a, um bloody
exsomnis, e sleepless
10 *exaudiri, historic inf.* reach the ear, hear
gemitus, us, m groan
verber, eris, n whipping, lashing
stridor, oris, m clanking, grating
catena, ae, f chain
strepitus, us, m din, noise
exterritus, a, um struck with terror
haurio, ire, hausi experience
scelus, eris, n crime
facies, ei, f type, form
effare, imperative speak
urgeo, ere crush, overwhelm
plangor, oris, m wailing, lamentation

15 *orsa (est)* began
fraus, fraudis, f deceit, fraud: a patron was bound by legal and sacred obligation to protect his client's interests
invideo, ere, vidi, visum hate
innecto, ere, nexui, nexus devise
divitiae, arum, f. pl. riches, wealth
incubo, are, ui keep a jealous watch
repertus, a, um acquired
20 *impius, a, um* unnatural, unholy: the epithet is regularly applied to civil war
fallo, ere fail to keep, break
dextra, ae, f pledge of trust
forma (poenae)
mergo, ere, mersi bury
quam poenam (exspectant)
volvo, ere roll: Sisyphus was doomed to roll uphill a stone that always fell back
radius, i, m spoke
rota, ae, f wheel
25 *destrictus, a, um* stretched out
pendeo, ere hang over, be suspended
Phlegyas Phlegyas represents the sin of sacrilege because he set fire to Apollo's temple at Delphi in Greece
testor, ari, atus sum call to witness
temno, ere scorn, disdain, despise
30 *fixit...refixit* Tr. "posted new laws and nullified them for a price"
thalamus, i, m bedroom
invado, ere, invasi, invasus invade
nata, ae, f daughter
vetitus, a, um forbidden
hymenaei, orum, m. pl. marriage
immanis, e monstrous
nefas, n, indecl. crime, abomination
potior, iri, potitus sum + abl. gain, obtain
35 *percurro, ere* run over, recount

ELYSIUM

    his demum exactis, perfecto munere divae,
devenere locos laetos et amoena virecta
fortunatorum nemorum sedesque beatas.
largior hic campos aether et lumine vestit
purpureo, solemque suum, sua sidera norunt.   5
pars in gramineis exercent membra palaestris,
contendunt ludo et fulva luctantur harena;
pars pedibus plaudunt choreas et carmina dicunt.
nec non Threicius longa cum veste sacerdos
obloquitur numeris septem discrimina vocum,   10
iamque eadem digitis, iam pectine pulsat eburno.
hic genus antiquum Teucri, pulcherrima proles,
magnanimi heroes nati melioribus annis,
Ilusque Assarcusque et Troiae Dardanus auctor.
arma procul currusque virum miratur inanes;   15
stant terra defixae hastae passimque soluti
per campum pascuntur equi quae gratia currum
armorumque fuit vivis. quae cura nitentes
pascere equos, eadem sequitur tellure repostos.
conspicit, ecce, alios dextra laevaque per herbam   20
vescentis laetumque choro paeana canentes
inter odoratum lauris nemus, unde superne
plurimus Eridani per silvam volvitur amnis.
hic manus ob patriam pugnando vulnera passi,
quique sacerdotes casti, dum vita manebat,   25
quique pii vates et Phoebo digna locuti,
inventas aut qui vitam excoluere per artes
quique sui memores aliquos fecere merendo:
omnibus his nivea cinguntur tempora vitta.

                              Lines 637-665

Elysium

After describing Tartarus to Aeneas at a fork in the road, the Sibyl conducts Aeneas down the road to Elysium, a place of brilliant sunshine.

---

exigo, ere, egi, actus complete
perficio, ere, feci, fectus perform
munus, eris, n offering (i.e., the Golden Bough)
diva, ae, f goddess (i.e., Proserpina, wife of Pluto)
amoenus, a, um pleasant
virecta, orum, n. pl. lawns
nemus, oris, n grove, wood
sedes, is, f abode, resting place
beatus, a, um blessed, fortunate
largus, a, um ample
aether, eris, m upper air, ether
lumen, inis, n light
vestio, ire clothe
5 *purpureus, a, um* bright, dazzling
norunt = noverunt know
gramineus, a, um grassy
membrum, i, n limb
palaestra, ae, f wrestling ground
fulvus, a, um yellow, tawny
luctor, ari wrestle
harena, ae, f sand
plaudo, ere beat out
chorea, ae, f dance
nec non likewise
Threicius...sacerdos the Thracian priest Orpheus, patron of music
10 *obloquitur numeris* Tr. "play as an accompaniment to the rhythm"
discrimina vocum Tr. "distinct notes"
digitus, i, m finger
pecten, inis, m plectrum, pick: used to strike the lyre's strings
eburnus, a, um ivory
Teucer, cri, m Teucer, an early King of Troy
proles, is, f race, line
magnanimus, a, um high-souled
Ilus, Assarcus Ilus was the grandfather of Priam, and Assarcus the grandfather of Anchises

Dardanus, i, m Dardanus, son of Jupiter and founder of Troy
15 *inanis, e* ghostly, phantom
passim everywhere, here and there
solutus, a, um unharnessed
quae gratia + gen. Tr. "whatever pleasure in"
nitens, entis sleek, well-groomed
pasco, ere feed; passive = graze
repono, ere, reposui, repostus lay to rest
20 *herba, ae, f* grass
vescor, vesci feed upon
chorus, i, m choir
paean, anis, m paean: a hymn of praise originally in honour of Apollo
odoratus, a, um fragrant
unde from which source
superne in the world above
plurimus Tr. "in all its strength"
Eridanus, i, m Eridanus River is the Padus (Po), which is fabled to flow from a source in the underworld
volvitur Tr. "rolls"
amnis, is, m river
hic (est) manus (eorum qui)... vulnera passi (sunt)
25 *quique (erant) sacerdotes*
castus, a, um pure
vates, is, m or f poet
et (verba) Phoebo digna locuti (sunt)
Phoebus, i, m Apollo
dignus, a, um + abl. worthy
excoluere = excoluerunt enriched, improved
merendo Tr. "by service done"
niveus, a, um snow white
cingo, ere surround, encircle
tempora, um, n. pl. temples (of the head), brow
vitta, ae, f fillet

The Pageant of Heroes

"huc geminas nunc flecte acies, hanc aspice gentem
Romanosque tuos. hic Caesar et omnis Iuli
progenies magnum caeli ventura sub axem.
hic vir, hic est, tibi quem promitti saepius audis,
Augustus Caesar, divi genus, aurea condet   5
saecula qui rursus Latio regnata per arva
Saturno quondam, super et Garamantas et Indos
proferet imperium; iacet extra sidera tellus,
extra anni solisque vias, ubi caelifer Atlas
axem umero torquet stellis ardentibus aptum. . . .   10
excudent alii spirantia mollius aera
(credo equidem), vivos ducent de marmore vultus,
orabunt causas melius, caelique meatus
describent radio et surgentia sidera dicent:
tu regere imperio populos, Romane, memento   15
(hae tibi erunt artes), pacique imponere morem,
parcere subiectis et debellare superbos."

                                        Lines 788-797; 847-853

The Gates of Sleep

   sunt geminae Somni portae, quarum altera fertur
cornea, qua veris facilis datur exitus umbris,
altera candenti perfecta nitens elephanto,
sed falsa ad caelum mittunt insomnia Manes.
his ibi tum natum Anchises unaque Sibyllam   5
prosequitur dictis portaque emittit eburna,
ille viam secat ad naves sociosque revisit.

                                        Lines 893-899

The Pageant of Heroes

In Elysium, Aeneas and the Sibyl meet Anchises who points out to his son Aeneas the famous Romans awaiting birth, such as Romulus, Caesar, and Augustus, and describes the nature of Rome's mission to the world.

---

geminus, a, um two
flecto, ere turn
acies, ei, f eye
progenies, ei, f descendant
ventura, fut. part. Tr. "destined to come"
axis, is, m vault
5 *divus, i, m* god (i.e., the deified Julius Caesar)
genus, eris, n offspring, son (i.e., Augustus)
condo, ere found, establish
saeculum, i, n generation, age
arvum, i, n field
Saturnus, i, m Saturn is the god who ruled Latium in the Golden Age
Garamantas, Gk. acc. the Garamantes, a North African tribe subdued by the Romans in 19 B.C., are used here to represent the southern extent of Augustus' empire
Indi, orum, m. pl. Indians: used here to represent remote Eastern peoples and regions
profero, proferre extend
extra + acc. beyond
sidus, eris, n star
caelifer, fera, ferum sky-bearing
Atlas, antis, m Atlas, the fabled giant who held up the sky

10 *torqueo, ere* cause to rotate, spin
stella, ae, f star
ardens, entis fiery, burning
aptus, a, um studded, fitted
excudo, ere shape, hammer out
spirans, spirantis breathing (i.e., lifelike)
mollius, adv. in more flowing lines
aes, aeris, n bronze
duco, ere mould, fashion
vivus, a, um living
marmor, oris, n marble
vultus, us, m face
oro, are plead, argue
caeli meatus Tr. "the movements of the heavenly bodies"
describo, ere mark out, map
radius, i, m measuring rod
15 *rego, ere* rule
imperium, ii, n government
memento = imperative form of *memini* remember
tibi dat. of possession
impono, ere establish
morem Tr. "a civilizing way of life"
parco, ere + dat. spare
subiectus, a, um the conquered
debello, are tame in war, subdue

The Gates of Sleep

Aeneas, who began his underworld journey often despondent, hesitant, and unsure, now ends his journey by departing through the ivory gate more confident and resolute in purpose.

---

fertur = dicitur is represented as
corneus, a, um made of horn
candens, ente shining, white
elephantus, i, m ivory
insomnium, ii, n dream

5 *Manes, ium, m. pl.* spirits of the dead
una together
eburnus, a, um ivory
viam secat makes his way

PART IV: A JOURNEY THROUGH THE UNDERWORLD

Initial Questions

The Descent to the Underworld
1. How does Vergil make the reader sense the unseen terrors of the ordeal that lies ahead for Aeneas?
2. What talisman must Aeneas find before he can see the regions not allowed to the living?
3. Show how Vergil uses diction, parallelism, anaphora, and asyndeton to create and sustain the tone of the passage.

The Portals of Hades
1. How do Vergil's choice of words, his juxtaposition of nouns and adjectives, and his use of simile and alliteration (lines 1 to 5) emphasize the emptiness, loneliness, and darkness of Hades?
2. What are the significant truths that Vergil is seeking to impart in describing and personifying the insubstantial qualities of ghosts and human fears? How effective is his use of personification in sustaining the tone of the passage?
3. What physical features make the following monsters horrifying: *Centauri, Scylla, Briareus, belua Lernae, Chimaera, Gorgones, Harpyiae,* and *forma tricorporis umbrae*?
4. Why does Vergil include the tree of dreams in his description?

Charon, Ferryman of the Dead
1. What Latin words, besides *horrendus*, describe Charon's grotesque but lifelike appearance?
2. Comment on the suitability of the following words: *ferruginea* (line 6), *viridis* (line 7), *stabant* (line 16), and *tendebant* (line 17).
3. Examine the two similes in this passage for their appropriateness, beauty, and deeper meaning. Which comparison best fits the spirits of the dead? Why? Can you suggest other appropriate similes to fit the description?
4. How does Vergil arouse our pity for the prospective passengers for Charon's boat?
5. How effective is Vergil's use of a "panning in" technique in portraying this scene?

Cerberus
1. Is Cerberus terrifying? comical? Why?
2. How does Aeneas get by Cerberus?
3. Explain the depth of meaning of *inremeabilis* in line 9.

Tartarus
1. How do Vergil's words, sounds, and images combine to provide a mood of gloom and sorrow and a grim setting for Tartarus?
2. Outline the various tortures of the damned in Tartarus.
3. *Pietas* is defined as a threefold duty to family, country, and gods. Are Vergil's categories of sin offences against *pietas*? Do the categories apply not only to Vergil's contemporaries but also to us today?

Elysium
1. Consider how Vergil uses imagery, diction, juxtaposition, alliteration (line 5), and onomatopoeia (line 8) to reflect the mood of happiness and the beauty of Elysium.
2. Which individuals and groups of individuals were allowed into the Groves of the Blessed?
3. Are the activities described in this idyllic scene attractive?
4. What do you suppose is the poet's purpose in this passage?

The Pageant of Heroes
1. How effective is Vergil's use of hyperbole and other poetic devices in this passage?
2. What is the significance of the geographical references in line 7?
3. Name and account for the respective skills and achievements of the Greeks and Romans.
4. What is the Roman mission and destiny expressed patriotically by Anchises? Do you think Anchises is speaking to Aeneas alone or to each future Roman?
5. Is Vergil delicately reminding Augustus of his responsibility to see that Rome's destiny is fulfilled?

The Gates of Sleep
1. Why did the Sibyl and Aeneas leave by the Ivory Gate?
2. Does this exit compare with the way they entered the underworld? Explain your answer.

Discussion Questions
1. Compare and contrast the different regions of the underworld under the following descriptions:
   (a) pathos, sorrow, and gloom of the past versus the hope, glory, peace, and serenity of the future;
   (b) sin (Tartarus) versus virtue (Elysium);
   (c) darkness versus light.
2. Which lines best sum up the character of each region? Explain the reasons for your choice.
3. Vergil's description of Aeneas' journey through the underworld is sufficiently detailed and graphic to be made into a film or a series of paintings. Do you agree? If you were making a movie or painting a picture, what would you select, emphasize, and add in your creation to appeal to your viewer?
4. How does Vergil envisage the afterlife? How do you?
5. What is the chief difference between Vergil's "Elysium" and Homer's "Elysium" (*cf. Odyssey* IV.560-568)
6. What is Vergil's vision of Rome and the type of citizen who should be part of Augustus' new order?
7. How did the experience of travelling through the underworld affect Aeneas' character?
8. Reread the selections from the *Aeneid* in this book and determine Vergil's technical skills as outlined in the biographical sketch on page xv and his ability to speak to his fellow countrymen and today's reader about the universal problems of human behaviour.

Further Readings

Aeneas is guided by the doves of his mother, Venus, to the Golden Bough, located on a tree near the crater entrance before Lake Avernus: Vergil, *Aeneid* VI.183-211.

Aeneas meets the shade of Dido in the Fields of Mourning: Vergil, *Aeneid* VI.450-476.

Anchises explains the doctrine of the transmigration of souls: Vergil, Aeneid VI.703-751.